무예도

무예도

발행일	2020년 5월 11일

지은이	양성오		
펴낸이	손형국		
펴낸곳	(주)북랩		
편집인	선일영	편집	강대건, 최예은, 최승헌, 김경무, 이예지
디자인	이현수, 한수희, 김민하, 김윤주, 허지혜	제작	박기성, 황동현, 구성우, 장홍석
마케팅	김회란, 박진관, 장은별		
출판등록	2004. 12. 1(제2012-000051호)		
주소	서울특별시 금천구 가산디지털 1로 168, 우림라이온스밸리 B동 B113~114호, C동 B101호		
홈페이지	www.book.co.kr		
전화번호	(02)2026-5777	팩스	(02)2026-5747

ISBN	979-11-6539-197-3 03690 (종이책)		979-11-6539-198-0 05690 (전자책)

이 도서의 국립중앙도서관 출판예정도서목록(CIP)은 서지정보유통지원시스템 홈페이지(http://seoji.nl.go.kr)와
국가자료공동목록시스템(http://www.nl.go.kr/kolisnet)에서 이용하실 수 있습니다.
(CIP제어번호: CIP2020018676)

무예도

MOO YEA DO

The Way of Discipline Art

양성오 지음
Dr. Tiger Yang

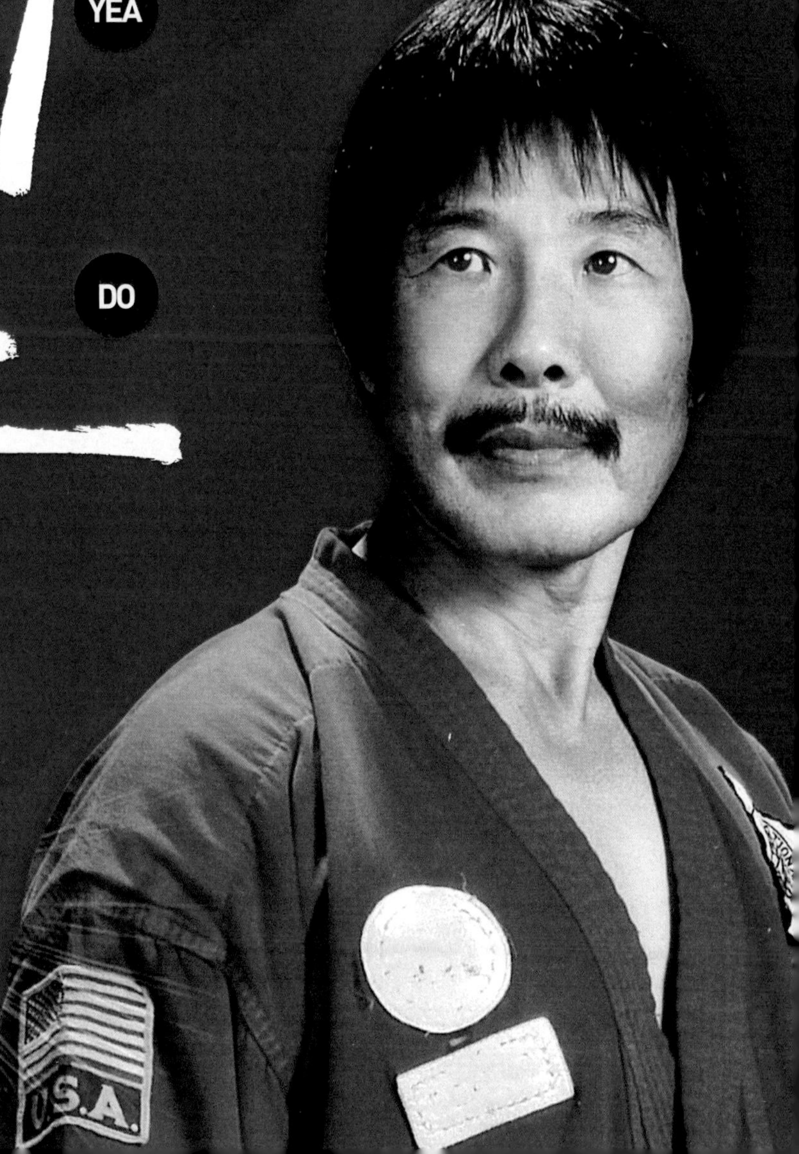

북랩 book Lab

차례

MOO YEA DO

타이거(성오) 양은
누구인가?

1944년 경북 경주에서 태어난 그는 어린 시절 일찍이 무덕관에 입문하여 혹독한 수련을 통하여 최연소 유단자로서 두각을 나타낸 후 성장하여 1970년 미국으로 건너가 태권도를 보급하는 데 공헌을 하였으며(시카고 6개 도장 운영) 1977년 제3회 세계 태권도 시카고 대회에서 공동준비 위원장으로 공헌하였다.

여러 번 텔레비전에 출연하여 태권도와 차력을 시범을 보여 인기를 얻은 후 Johnny Carson Show 그리고 That'S Incredibles 전국 T.V에 출연하여 200파운드 역기를 입으로 물고 걷고 8톤 트럭에 50명을 태우고 밧줄을 묶어 이빨로 물어 끌고 6장 쌓아 올린 키 높이의 얼음을 격파하는 시범을 보여 전국적인 명성을 얻었다. 그 후 그는 여러 나라에서 초청을 받아 시범 공연을 하였다.

1976년 무하마드 알리와 인연을 맺고 일본 도쿄에서 있었던 알리와 이노끼 시합에 알리 트레이너로 동행한 후 알리와 같이 한국과 필리핀을 방문하였다. 홍콩으로 건너가 골든하베스트 영화사와 8편의 계약을 하고 촬영을 끝낸 후 대만 국영 TV 초청으로 연속극에 출연하였으며 영화, 각종 TV 프로그램에 출연하여 최고의 전성기(한류 원조)를 보냈다. 그는 영화 30여 편에 출연하면서 연기를 하기 위하여 중국 무술을 열심히 배웠다. 그는 1980년 할리우드 영화사 United Cinema Feature와 계약을 하고 돌아와 Operation Overkill, Death Penalty, Mission Kill Fast, Omega Assassins, Master Incredibles 에 출연하였고 1994년 The Internatioanl AB Flex Commercial(C.F) 에 출연하였다. 그리하여 그는 1980년 태권도, 쿵후, 합기도의 장점들. 예를 들어 태권도 발차기, 쿵후의 빠른 손동작, 합기도의 상대 중심 이용 및 꺾기를 하나로 집약시켜 무예도란 새로운 류를 창시하여 미 연방정부(95-3766894)에 1981년 9월 17일 등록하였다 무엇보다 무예도는 예와 인격을 중시한다.

그는 태권도 9단, 무예도 10단이다. 베트남전에도 참전하여 태권도를 보급하였으며 미국에 서는 미 CIA 시카고 일리노이 경찰학교에서 무도를 지도하였고 2017년 무도 명예전당에 입성하였다.

그는 무예도를 만든 창시자, 도주 그리고 국제무예도 연맹 총재로서 후진양성에 매진하고 있다.

 MOO YEA DO

무예도란 무엇인가?

먼 옛날부터 끊임없이 이어져 내려오는 자연의 흐름이란 불멸의 진리이다. 인류 사회에서 필요에 의하여 만들어진 것이라도 바탕에 확고한 진리가 있다면 그 흐름의 상하가 있다 하더라도 살아서 숨 쉬며 발전하는 그 법칙에는 변함이 없는 것이다. 오랜 세월을 두고 사람들의 생활 속에 (민족) 계승되어온 무술도 본바탕이 되는 진리를 잊어버리지 않는 한 계속 이어져 참된 인간 생활의 표본이 되고 질서 있는 사회를 만드는 존경심이 기술보다 중히 여겨야 함이 이어져 가야 한다. 무예도는 오랜 역사 속에 전해 내려온 여러 류의 기술을 29년의 태권도(9단) 수련의 경력 및 실전 경험과 무술액션 영화(30편)에 출연하면서 다년간 수련한 쿵후, 합기도와 태권도의 장점을 현대인들에게 맞도록 기술을 1980년에 개발하여 미국 연방정부에 등록한 새로운 종합무술이다.

특히나 정신교육, 체력단련과 전 세계의 많은 사람들이 무예도 수련을 통하여 평화롭고 아름다운 질서 있는 무도인 사회를 건설하고자 하는 데 창시의 목적이 있다. 그러므로 독특한 기본동작을 정신과 육체가 하나가 되어 수련하므로 그 도의 진가를 터득하게 되며 실생활에 활용하여 살아있는 동안 마음에 평안과 육체의 건강을 유지하게 되는 것이며 무도의 수련은 하루아침에 이루어지는 것이 아니다. 오랜 시간 같은 동작을 반복 연습하므로 그 진가를 터득하게 되며 무도 수련은 천재가 없다. 오직 수련만이 달인이 되는 것이다. 이 책 한 권이 여러분의 인생에 큰 도움이 되었으면 하는 것이 필자의 소망이다.

무예도의 특수한 원리는 무엇인가?

무슨 일이든 이해하고 익숙해지려면 그 특수한 원리를 정확히 파악할 필요가 있다. 무예도의 특수한 원리는 정신의 움직임에 있다.

정신의 움직임은 자연의 법칙에 있고 자연에 순응하여 움직이는 힘. 그것은 곧 정신에서 나온다. 그러므로 정신이 모든 육체를 움직인다는 것은 무예도의 원리인 것이다. 무예도 움직임 모두가 정신의 움직임으로부터 발하는 파장이고 그 원리가 곧 자연의 움직임에 순응하는 기가 담겨 있다. 그러므로 무예도의 정신 움직임은 우주 그 자체이며 원의 중심에서 일어나는 파장이다.

무예도의 움직임이야말로 우주의 진리에 근원을 둔 정신 움직임을 현대 문화에 적응시킨 심신단련의 수련이다. 정신의 움직임을 무예도의 근원에 둔 것은 정신 그리고 육체의 움직임과 모든 우주 생성의 진리를 파악할 수 있는 힘. 곧 상대를 움직일 수 있는 힘. 그것이 곧

정신에서 나오므로 무예도의 원리는 정신 움직임이며 그 수련 방법
도 육체보다 정신의 움직임을 단련하고 'ㄱ' 기법을 터득하여 단련하
여야 한다.

무예도의 조화(합리)

　무예도의 움직임은 정신과 육체의 조화이다. 정신의 움직임이 곧 육체의 움직임으로 이루어진다. 그러므로 정신의 움직임에서 파장되는 모든 동작에서 일어나는 힘의 강약을 조절할 수 있으며 그 조절이 곧 정신의 움직임이다. 예를 들어 상대를 제압하기 위하여 주먹을 뻗을 때 팔꿈치에서 정면으로 지르는 짧은 거리에서 생성하는 힘을 상대의 몸체에 닫기 전 힘의 강약을 조절하는 운동이야말로 현대 생활에서 정신과 육체의 피곤에서 오는 스트레스를 풀어주는 맑은 정신을 가질 수 있는 기의 순환 운동이며 기(에너지)에서 발생하는 에너지로 육체를 단련하고 노화를 방지하면서 몸의 구석구석까지 혈의 흐름을 도와 육체를 튼튼하게 해준다.

정신의 움직임으로 집중력 강화

무예도는 근접 거리에서 일어나는 모든 동작을 일으키는 순간, 부딪치는 곳에서 변화된 움직임으로 그 기법을 터득하고 정신의 움직임으로 상대의 기의 흐름에 따라 생성하는 기를 양성해야 한다. 그렇지만 우리는 일상생활에 필요한 도를 수련하여 상대를 인정하고 존중하며 예를 갖춰 상대를 대할 때 비로소 도를 수련하는 수련자라 할 것이다.

철저하게 일어나는 모든 행동을 합리적으로 승화시켜 나가기란 그리 쉬운 일은 아니다. 그래서 끊임없는 수련을 요하게 되는 것이다. 자기의 수련을 충분히 활용할 때 일어나는 기의 현상으로 과히 믿기 어려운 힘을 발휘하게 되는 것이다. 예를 들면 어린 자식이 지프차 뒷바퀴에 깔리려는 순간 목숨을 구하기 위하여 그 어머니가 뒷바퀴를 번쩍 들어 목숨을 구하는 일이란 상상을 초월한 정신의 움직임이 집체

하여 설 때 일어난 현상이다. 그와 같이 정신과 육체가 조화를 이루었을 때 그 집중력이 발휘된 것이다. 누구든지 무예도의 정신 움직임을 수련하면 언제든지 생각하는 대로 그 힘을 낼 수 있는 것이다.

무예도가 왜 현대인에게 필요한가

　무예도가 옛날 사회의 무도 같이 자기방어, 가족 그리고 나라를 방위하기 위한 힘 겨룸의 무술이라면 무의 정의 하나로도 충분할 것이다. 허나 현대인들의 생활 속에 깊숙이 파고들어 건강과 맑은 정신을 추구하기 위한 운동이어야 하며 그러기 위하여 예를 중시하고 바른 길로 가기 위한 예와 도의 연마야말로 단순한 무도가 아닌 심신 단련의 도로써 우리 현대인들에게 필요한 요소라 할 수가 있다.

사회적 필요조건

무예도가 종래의 무도같이 현대 문명 이전에 무예를 겨루고 힘과 기술을 시험하는 무술에 머물러 있었다면 소수인으로 제한되고 일반적인 근대 생활과는 무관한 것으로 생각되었을 것이다. 하지만 무예도의 본질과 요소는 존경, 책임,명예를 본질로 하고 건강한 정신, 건강한 육체, 정직한 마음을 요소로 단련하여 하나로 결집한 운동의 결정체이므로 무예도가 근대 생활 속에 뿌리 깊게 침투하는 것이며 단순한 무도가 아닌 심신단련의 도로서 현대인의 필요에 의한 요소가 되는 까닭이라 생각된다.

따라서 무도로서의 가치를 인정받고 근대 생활의 일부로서 확고한 바탕을 구축하자면 시대에 맞는 기술이 개발되어야 된다. 앞에서도 말했지만 무예도는 오랜 무술의 전통에서 태권도, 쿵후, 합기도의 다양한 기술을 현대인들에게 맞도록 한 단계 차원을 높인 종합 무술이다. 그러므로 무예도 동작은 무도 기술의 수련에 있지만 그 단련은 마음을 중심으로 하여 육체가 하나가 되어 심심 통일의 극치를 무도적으로 어떤 방법으로 터득하는가에 있으므로 그 근원은 기. 심. 체로 이루어진다. 첫째로 기는 무예도에서 가장 강조되고 있는 것이며 언제나 기를 무한히 그리고 힘차게 내도록 해야 한다. 기의 의미는 인간 행동의 근원을 가리키며 우주 대자연의 기와 일체가 되었을 때 비로소 무한의 힘이 발휘되는 것이다.

MOO YEA DO

무예도와
생활

무예도 창시자 타이거 양 도주는 무예도로서 전 세계 사람들이 건강하고 평화를 사랑하며 화합하고 인류의 평화가 달성되었으면 좋겠다고 말했다. 이것은 무예도 단련의 필수적으로 자기와 우주의 기(에너지)가 하나 됨을 목표로 정하고 자기의 몸(작은 우주)에 자연과의 조화를 만들어내는 데 있다는 것을 말한 것이다. 이러한 자연의 극치를 그려내면 움직임이 어디까지나 합리적인 조화라 무리한 부딪침이 전혀 없게 되고 상대와 자연히 조화를 이루는 극치에 달하게 된다. 이와 같이 무예도의 근본정신이 있기 때문에 짧은 역사를 가진 무예도가 캘리포니아를 중심으로 각 주 그리고 세계로 보급되고 있으며 인종의 구별 없이 화합을 이루어 행복한 삶 그 자체가 무예도의 생활이라고 할 수 있다. 무예도에 있어서 기를 터득하고 이것을 활용할 수 있으면 일상생활에서 무슨 일이든 자기가 갖고 있는 힘을 충분히 발휘하여 활용할 수가 있다.

둘째로 마음인데 무예도의 연마는 언제고 마음이 중심이 되며 마음의 연마는 기의 연마에 의한 자연에 순응하는 조화의 추구와 서로 연관되어 무도의 본질이라 할 수 있는 성실, 용기, 정직, 예절과 같은 미덕이 자연 조화를 이룬다.

셋째, 몸인데 무예도의 육체의 단련은 자연(우주)과 일치가 된 합리성과 연결되고 그 동작은 강인하고 부드러우며 또한 일어나는 반사적 동작이 재빠르게 움직임으로 일어나므로 건강이나 자기방어를 위해서도 좋다. 이 모든 동작들은 현대인의 삶에 있어 무예도의 역할이란 참으로 중요한 것이다.

 MOO YEA DO

기법 원리적 특질

무예도를 통한 수행에 의해서 비로소 몸에 터득이 된다. 이것을 서구식으로 분석 해석하려면 곤란하다. 이러한 것이 바로 동양에서 발생한 동양 무술, 즉 도의 본질이라 할 수 있을 것이다. 그러나 동양적인 도를 터득하려는 사람들을 도와주고 이끌어 주기 위한 설명이 절대적으로 필요한 것이다 그러면 무예도의 힘의 근원이라 할 수 있는 기(에너지)에 관해서 설명하고 기에 의해 만들어지는 무예도의 동작을 오늘날의 역학적 관점에서 입증하겠다.

무예도의 기의 파악

기에 대한 사고방식은 사람에 따라 약간 다르다. 그것은 각자의 체험이 다르기 때문이다. 기는 동양적인 말이다. 옛날 문헌에는 자주 등장하여 여러 가지의 의미로 쓰이고 있다. 철학적인 의미로 쓰이고 있는가 하면 순전히 생리적인 뜻으로도 쓰이고 있다. 그러므로 여기서는 어떤 정의를 내리기보다는 어디까지나 수련을 통해서 몸으로 터득하라고 하고 싶다. 기는 크게 말하자면 대자연 발생 근원이고 작게는 인간 생명력의 근원이다. 바꾸어 말하자면 이 우주의 생명력을 인간이 그 육체를 통해서 흡수하는 것인데 단순히 호흡하는 것이 아니라 수련에 의해 보다 큰 생명력으로 발휘하자는 것이다. 그것이 바로 도장에서 무예도를 연마함으로써 우리가 얻고자 하는 목적이며 자연과 일치된 기법이 무예도의 이상이라 할 수 있다.

무예도 창시자 타이거 양은 일찍이 기는 무예도라고 말했다. 이것은 간단한 말이지만 또한 깊은 뜻이 내포되어 있다. 앞에서 말한 기의 철학적인 의미와 생리적인 의미를 아울러 생각할 때 어렴풋이 짐작이 되리라 생각된다.

하여간 기를 파악하고 그것을 자유롭게 쓸 수 있게 하기 위해서는 매일 같이 수련에 전진해야 할 것이다. 이것이 곧 수행이다. 그러나 그 수행도 잘못된 것이면 기를 터득하고 자유롭게 행사할 수가 없다. 그렇다면 올바른 수행이란 어떤 것인가?

무예도의 기법을 단련하는 마음가짐으로는 첫째, 인간의 중심에 들어앉은 단전에 마음을 가라앉힐 것. 상대를 극히 자연스럽게 힘을 주지 않는 유연한 상태로 만들 것. 상대편이 있어도 그것에 조금도 구애받지 않을 것. 이상의 세 가지를 생각해야 한다. 둘째로는 언제나 단전을 중심으로 양 수도를 통해 뿜어지는 자기의 기에 힘이 모아지도록 할 것이며 이 힘을 무예도의 독특한 원운동에 의해서 처리하면서 기술을 터득하고 기력을 자유롭게 움직여 그 터득을 확고한 것으로 만들어가야 하는 것이다.

기(에너지)의 흐름

자연계의 모든 것에 기가 있으며 가득 차 있다. 그 기가 활동하는 이상을 기의 흐름이라 한다. 부모의 원수를 만났을 때 검술의 기술이 보통인 자가 눈을 감고 필사적으로 찌르기를 하여 검술에 통달한 사람을 쓰러뜨렸다는 이야기가 전해지고 있다. 이것은 인간이 무아지경에 들어갔을 때 승패를 초월한 절대 부동의 마음에서 발하는 기의 흐름이 상대편을 압도시킨 하나의 좋은 보기이다.

그 어떤 것에도 사로잡히지 않고 요동하지 않으며 임기응변으로 자기 본체에서 자연히 폭발하는 힘을 기의 흐름이라 한다. 어떤 유명한 검술에 통달한 사람은 이렇게 기술했다. "온다면 이것을 맞이하고 간다면 이것을 보낸다." 맞선다면 화한다. 오오는 열이다. 이팔도 열이다. 일구도 열이다. 그러므로 이로써 화하는 것이다. 이것은 기의 흐름을 쫓아 몸을 대응시켜 나간다는 것으로써 상대가 오기를 기다렸

다가 맞이하고 그런 다음에 보낸다는 뜻이 아니라 상대로 하여금 오지 않으면 안 될 심정에까지 몰아넣고 이것을 처리해 간다는 검술의 비법을 설명한 것이다. 이와 같은 기의 흐름은 하루하루의 바른 수련을 반복함으로써 그 경지에 마침내 도달할 수가 있는 것이다.

기(에너지), 심(마음), 체(몸)의 일체

　기를 스스로 터득하고 이것을 충분히 구사하는 것이 얼마나 중요하며 또한 어렵다는 것을 이미 말했다. 그러나 기의 활용으로 무한한 힘을 내고자 할 때 기. 심. 체가 제멋대로 흩어져 있다면 아무것도 아니다. 기가 심기를 일으키고 마음이 몸을 움직이는 만큼 그 통일이 결여된다면 매우 부자연스러운 결과가 되고 만다. 인간이 심부전에 의해 갑자기 죽어버리듯 인간 실격이 될 수도 있다.

　오래전부터 불교에서는 좌선법이 성행되고 있었듯이 도라고 이름 붙인 것은 그 나름의 고심을 하고 있는 것이다. 무예도에서는 이 통일체를 스스로 터득하고 스스로 나타내기 위해서 나날의 단련이 계속되고 있는 것이다. 상대를 자기의 일부처럼 조종하면서 기법을 나타낼 수 있게끔 연마하고 만일 그것이 달성되었다면 그때는 종교에서 말하는 깨우침으로 눈물에 젖은 경지가 될 것이며 기. 심. 체의 통일로써 무한한 힘을 발휘할 수 있는 상태가 될 것이다. 따라서 언제 어디에 있거나 어떤 경우에 처하더라도 기. 심. 체가 일치된 무한한 힘을 발휘할 수 있게 수련을 해야만 할 것이다. 이런 상태를 무예도 수련의 목표로 삼아야 될 것이다.

 MOO YEA DO

기본자세와 보법

신체단련과 실전에 응용되는 자세

무예도에서는 굳이 어떤 형을 필수로 하지 않는다. 그러나 초보자의 수련 편리상 몇 가지를 정하여 자세를 가다듬는데 사용하며 초보자에게는 기초과정으로써 하체와 상체 및 허리 부위의 단련을 위하여 형에 의한 자세를 반복수련시키고 있다.

신체는 지면에 양다리를 짚고서야 제대로 힘을 발휘할 수가 있다 손과 팔이 있는 상체가 아무리 튼튼히 발달하여 좋은 기술을 갖고 있다 하더라도 지면을 짚고 있는 하체가 약하다면 힘을 낼 수 있는 지반이 없으므로 단련된 힘을 쓸 수가 없는 것이다.

무예도에서는 단을 획득하기까지 무예 기본형부터 무예 8까지의 형을 필수 이수해야 하며 이외에도 각자의 수련 목적과 체질에 따라 주어지는 여러 가지의 기술을 수련해야 하고 정신의 힘을 기르기 위하여 백절불굴의 정신, 예절, 존경 및 정신 수양의 인격이 갖추어져

야 승단의 자격이 주어진다. 각력과 완력, 용력을 배양하기 위하여 꾸준히 수련한 사람은 반석과 같은 기반을 갖추게 되는 것이다.

무예도 형을 설명한다면 기본 1, 2, 3은 중심을 잡는 자세와 흔히 말하는 강권에 의한 수련을 하는 것이다. 무예 4, 5형은 자세의 변화와 허리의 뒤틀림이 많아지고 발차기가 수반되며 완력을 양성하여 몸의 유연성을 기르며 순발력과 도약력을 기르고 점차로 유권에 가까워진다. 무예 6형에는 손과 발을 같이 사용하여 스피드와 힘이 강조되고 격렬한 동작 후 단전호흡을 통하여 자세 및 힘을 축적하는 내공 단련과 좌우 측방 공격으로 상대를 제압하는 강한 기교가 첨가된다. 무예 7, 8형에는 다양한 자세 변화와 동작의 흐름으로 상대를 혼란케 하고 강권과 유권의 변화된 공격 및 방어로 허리의 유연성과 단전호흡을 통한 기를 축적하여 연속 공격의 피로를 적게 하고 순발력과 도약력을 기르며 정신과 육체의 화합을 이루는 수련이다. 여기에 각 수련생에게 맞도록 보조형이 추가되어 명실공히 실력자가 되도록 하며 상대를 공방하는 데 있어서 전사와 발경이 순조롭도록 유연성을 보이게 되고 무리한 동작이 없어 무도를 수련하는 기간을 연장하여 무도인으로서의 긍지와 젊음을 지속시켜 나가는 것이다.

기본자세

- ○ 기마자세
- ○ 전굴자세
- ○ 후굴자세
- ○ 대련자세
- ○ 가위자세
- ○ 선자세

기마자세

무예도의 기본자세이며 각 무도에서도 기본이 되는 필수적인 자세
로 무예도에서도 중요시하여 이 자세로 기 수련에 많은 효과를 얻고

있다. 양발을 말을 타는 자세와 같이 양쪽으로 어깨너비로 벌리고 발뿌리와 무릎 안쪽으로 15도 각도로 모으고 그대로 앉은 자세로 대퇴부 안쪽을 바깥쪽으로 밀어내듯이 한다. 무릎이 앞으로 약간 나오게 하고 발뒤꿈치 무릎 엉덩이에 힘을 모아 발뒤꿈치와 엉덩이 상체가 일직선 중심이 되도록 해야 한다. 낮은 자세를 취할 때 앞으로 수그러지며 턱을 당기고 단전호흡을 하여 힘을 모으고 숨을 고르게 하여 단전 부위에 기가 집중되도록 해야 한다.

전굴자세

크게 내딛는 걸음걸이와 같다 하여 걷는 자세라고도 한다. 준비자세(양쪽 어깨너비로 양발을 벌려 선 자세)에서 오른발을 한 걸음 내디딤과 동시 앞무릎이 45도로 굽혀져야 하며 동시에 70퍼센트 체중이 실려야 하고 왼쪽 다리는 쭉 뻗음과 동시에 몸의 중심 30퍼센트가 지탱된 자세이다. 이때 양쪽 발뿌리는 안쪽으로 향하게 한다. 양쪽 발바닥이 지면에서 떨어져선 안 되며 엉치뼈와 상체 뒷머리가 일직선으로 중심을 이루어야 한다. 이 자세는 다리를 강하게 하는 데 목적이 있으므로 다리에 힘을 넣어 허리가 삐뚤게 되지 않도록 한다. 상대를 공격해서 밀어내는데 필요한 자세이다.

후굴자세

이 자세는 한쪽 발에 전 체중을 싣고 한쪽 발은 가볍게 발끝만 지면에 닿게 한다. 그러므로 이 자세를 웅크린 고양이 모양과도 같다 하여 Cat Stance라고도 한다. 이 자세는 한쪽 발은 싣이고 한쪽 발은 허이기에 퇴력을 증가시키는 데 좋은 자세이며 앞쪽 발이 받어차기로 하단 공격에 유리하며 퇴보에는 빠르다. 이 자세는 특히 낭심 공격에 필히 취하는 자세이다.

대련자세(Wide Cat Stance)

준비자세에서 한쪽 발이 뒤로 나가 발끝이 약간 안쪽으로 향하게 하고 뒷무릎은 적당히 굽힌 자세가 되고 체중은 앞쪽 40 뒷발을 60으로 배분하는 것이 효율적이며 무예도에선 이 자세를 Wlde Cat Stance라고도 한다. 무예도에선 이 자세를 대련 자세로 하며 차고 지르는 동작, 상대가 공격해올 때 방어 그리고 막고 잡아당기며 좌우로 회전하며 변화하는 기술 숙달에 아주 편리한 자세이다.

가위자세

이 자세는 기마자세에서 좌 혹은 우로 상체를 돌려 중심을 잡고 앞쪽 발끝이 밖으로 45도로 돌리고 체중은 70퍼센트를 무릎으로 중심을 잡으며 뒷발꿈치를 들고 30퍼센트 체중을 지탱한다. 이때 안 대퇴부위는 접촉되어야 한다. 이 자세는 앞뒤의 상대를 몸을 틀어 공격, 방어할 수 있고 단전을 통하여 기를 모으고 변화무쌍한 공격을 할 수 있는 자세이므로 많은 수련을 통하여 얻어지는 기술이라 하겠다.

선자세

외다리로 중심을 잡고 서 있는 자세인데 서 있는 자세는 펴 있지만 뻣뻣해서는 안 되며 올린 다리는 무릎을 구부렸거나 발뿌리를 앞으로 향하기도 하고 땅을 향하기도 한다. 상체는 전후좌우 흔들림 없이 중심에 유의해야 하며 이 자세는 하단 후리기를 피하거나 발로 공격하며 들어갈 때 유용하게 쓰인다. 이외에도 많은 자세들이 있지만 많은 기술을 아는 것보다 한 가지 기술이라도 오랜 수련을 통하여 깊이 알고 응용하는 것이 최선이다. 오직 반복하는 수련만이 진정 무도인의 승자가 되는 길이다.

 MOO YEA DO

기 보충법 그리고
복식호흡법과 운동

기를 조절하는 방법

기(에너지)라는 말이 생소하더라도 사람들은 각각의 방법으로 기를 조정하거나 단련하고 있다. 노래를 부르거나 큰소리를 지르는 것도 (기합) 스트레스 발산에 도움이 되는 동시에 노래하고 큰 소리 지르는 것으로 숨을 강하게 내뱉고 거기에 따라서 기를 받아들이고 있는 것이다. 아무 데나 쓰러져 누워 있는 것도 피로를 회복하고 기를 충족시키는 효용이 있다고 말할 수 있고 책을 열심히 읽어 기를 조정하는 사람도 있다.

일요일마다 골프를 치지 않으면 기분이 이상해지는 사람, 정기적으로 무술도장에 나가 수련하지 않으면 자기 몸에서 흐르는 기가 고르지 못함을 느낀다. 땀과 스트레스를 발산하기 위해서 사우나를 이용하는 사람이 있는가 하면 계절에 관계없이 하루에 몇 마일씩 달리는 사람도 있다. 어느 것이나 기를 고르게 하는 방법 중에 하나이다. 어떤 방법이 좋은가는 일률적으로 정할 순 없다. 어떤 운동이 맞느냐는 개인의 차가 있기 때문이다. 평소 혈액순환이 잘 안 되는 사람은 달리는 것이 좋을 것이다. 조깅이나 마라톤은 기와 피의 순환을 좋게 하기 때문이다. 또 수분이 많은 사람은 상식적이지만 사우나 등에서 여분의 수분을 내보냄으로써 기를 고르게 하는 데 도움이 된다. 인간은 기. 혈. 수로 구성되고 그 균형이 깨지면 반 건강인에서 반 환자가 되고 얼마 지나지 않아 진짜 환자가 된다.

크게 나누어 기를 몸에서 보충하는 방법은 다음과 같다.

○ **기의 상태를 좋게 하는 방법**   **기의 건강법**
○ **혈(피) 의 상태를 좋게하는 방법**   **혈의 건강법**
○ **수(물) 상태를 좋게 하는 방법**   **수(물) 건강법**

기의 건강법

떠들어서 기분을 전환하거나 무도를 수련하며 기합을 크게 내거나 코미디(웃기는 소리)를 듣고 유쾌하게 웃거나 요가 수련, 복식 호흡 등 소리, 호흡에 관계되는 것이 중심이다.

혈(피)의 건강법

혈액순환을 좋게 하는 것으로 걷거나 뛰거나 마라톤, 무도 수련, 체조와 같이 몸을 움직여서 하는 방법이다. 목욕하는 것도 몸을 덥게 하여 혈액을 잘 순환하게 한다는 건 평소에 경험하는 것이다.

수(물)의 건강법

땀을 내는 방법이라면 무엇이라도 좋은 것이다. 대표적인 것에는 사우나가 있으나 보통의 목욕에서도 땀은 나오며 조깅이나 마라톤에서도 땀은 난다. 요컨대 모든 것이 기분전환을 위한 방법이다.

일에서 잠시 마음과 몸이 벗어나 소모된 기를 축적하는 것이다. 이것 중에 제일 쉬운 방법은 잡담일 것이다. 크게 소리 내어 웃지 않더라도 허물없는 대화는 매우 좋은 기분전환의 특효약인 것이다.

기분이 가라앉았을 때 한두 시간 떠들고 있는 동안에 완전히 원기가 솟아나 무엇을 하고자 하는 생각이 솟았다는 경험은 누구든지 기억하고 있을 것이다. 의식적으로 한패를 만들어 의논, 담소하거나 하는 일을 성미가 까다로운 사람들은 시간 낭비라 생각하지만 정보교환 이상으로 기의 건강법상으로 볼 때 좋은 일이다. 삶 속에서 실시하는 기분전환은 그때까지 기를 집중하고 있던 것으로부터 일단 떠나 다른 뭔가를 하는 것으로 달성된다. 관심의 대상을 바꾼다. 비일상적인 경험 그리고 직업에 대한 생각에서 노는 마음으로 바꾸는 연구의 방법은 천차만별이지만 부지 중에 누구나가 다하고 있는 것이다.

기를 몸으로 보충하는 방법으로써 더욱 의식적, 적극적으로 하는 데는 대량의 공기를 들이마시는 것으로 여기에는 더욱 적극적인 기의 건강법으로써 복식호흡, 조깅에 대해서 실시 방법과 효용에 관하여 언급해 보기로 하자.

복식호흡은 기를 충분히 몸 안에 받아들여 인간을 강하게 한다. 복식호흡에는 여러 가지 방법이 있다. 앞에서 언급한 것처럼 노래를 불러도 자연히 복식호흡이 되고 마라톤을 해도 그렇게 된다. 원리는 횡격막을 크게 밀어 내리고 밀어 올리며 하는 것이다. 어떤 호흡이든 횡격막은 움직이지만 중요한 것은 그 진폭의 크기이다. 여성은 남성에 비하여 횡격막이 위아래로 움직이는 폭이 작아 흉식호흡을 하고 있다고 말하는데 그만큼 횡격막이 움직이는 폭이 작은 것이다. 그 횡격막을 마음껏 위아래로 움직이는 복식호흡을 극단적인 형태로 해 보자는 것이 여기서 소개하는 방법이다 복식호흡에는 서양식 방법과 동양적인 단전호흡법이 있다. 우선 서양식의 복식호흡은 숨을 내쉴 때 배를 끌어당기며 숨을 들어쉴 때 배를 불룩하게 하는 호흡법으로 그렇게 함으로써 횡격막이 충분히 상하로 움직인다. 의자에 앉은 채로 또는 정좌하고 혹은 위로 보고 누워서도 할 수 있다.

그 목적은 어느 때보다 많은 기를 체내에 끌어들여 신진대사를 활발하게 하고자 하는 것이다. 우선 숨을 조용히 들이쉬면서 서서히 하복부를 팽창시켜가는 것이다. 배 전체가 아니고 배꼽 아래가 팽팽해지도록 한다. 계속해서 천천히 숨을 내쉬는 것인데 내쉬면서 하복부를 점점 오므려 가는 것이다. 가능한 긴 시간을 들이마시고 내쉬게 하는 것이 좋고 양손으로 하복부를 눌러 더욱 오므리면서 완전히 내뱉어 버리는 것이다. 숨을 들이마시는 데는 2~3초로 충분하지만 내쉴 때는 적어도 20 내지 30초간은 내쉬는 걸 계속하도록 반복한다. 최종적으로 일 분 정도를 목표로 하는 것이 좋을 것이다. 한 번에 3회를 반복하되 아침, 낮, 밤. 하루에 세 번씩 목표로 해보자.

다음에 단전호흡법을 소개하겠다. 서양식의 복식호흡은 숨을 내쉴 때 하복부에 강한 압력을 주는 호흡법이다. 그것에 의해서 평소와는 비교도 안 될 정도의 다량의 산소가 체내에 들어와 신진대사가 활발해진다. 간단한 단전호흡법은 이렇게 한다. 우선 앉거나 선다. 등을 똑바로 펴고 단전, 즉 배꼽 밑에 힘을 준다. 다음 어깨에 힘을 뺀다.

그러면 단전에만 힘이 들어가 있는 상태가 된다. 그 위에 상체를 쓰러뜨리면서 숨을 내쉰다. 최초에는 2, 3초부터 시작하여 익숙해지면 30초 정도 내쉰다. 다음에 상체를 일으키면서 숨을 들이마시는 것이다. 이와 같은 복식호흡을 훈련해 가는 도중에 일상적인 흉식호흡에서 복식호흡으로 전환되어 간다. 그런데 복식호흡은 뇌간을 단련한다고 말한다.

뇌간이란 것은 뇌 속에 제일 원시적이고 기본적인 부분으로 이곳을 단련하면 동물적인 강인한 마음, 즉 움직이지 않는 마음을 만든다고 말한다. 그리고 뇌관은 기와 큰 관계가 있는 부분이다.

복식호흡이 어째서 뇌간을 단련하는 것일까? 인체의 신경계는 의식하고 몸을 움직이는 수의 신경과 의식해도 움직일 수 없는 부수의 신경 자율 신경으로 나누어져 있다. 부수의 신경은 동물적인 뇌간에 가까운 곳에 중추가 있다. 내장을 움직이고 있는 자율신경은 뇌의 구피질(무의식, 감정 세계)로 지배되어 있어 심장이든 간장이든 우리가 잠자고 있든 깨어있든 부드럽게 움직이고 있다.

또 몸의 리듬 수면이나 각성, 호흡, 체온, 수분 조정 등을 재고 있는 것은 뇌간이라고 여겨진다. 부수의 신경은 뇌의 신피질, 의식, 지능의 세계에서는 직접 명령할 수 없는 구조로 되어있다. 예를 들면 신피질에서 의식하고 심장을 멈추려고 해도 불가능한 일이며 다른 장기도 그와 같다. 심장병도 의식하여 고칠 수가 없다. 호흡 중추는 부수의 신경도 지배하고 있어 원리적으로는 의식하여 호흡을 컨트롤할 수 없는 것이지만 훈련에 따라서는 어느 정도까지 컨트롤할 수가 있다. 지금 여기에 적은 것처럼 일 분 전후까지도 숨을 계속 내쉴 수 있다고 하는 것이 그 증거이다. 반대로 숨을 잠시 멈추고 있을 수 있다는 것은 누구나 알고 있다. 그런데 호흡 컨트롤에 숙달되면 수의 신경과 부수의 신경 관련이 좋아져서 부수의 신경도 점점 컨트롤할 수 있게 되는 변화가 생기는 것이다. 단전호흡에 충분히 숙달되면 그 여파로 심장까지도 어느 정도 컨트롤하는 일이 가능해지는 것이다. 심전도가 분명히 바뀐다. 물론 좋은 방향으로 변해오는 것이다. 심전도처럼 눈으로 보아 그 변화를 분명히 확인할 수 있는 것은 현재 심장밖에 없으므로 단언할 수는 없으나 아마 다른 장기에도 좋은 영향을 미치고 있다고 생각해도 틀림없다고 나는 생각한다. 예를 들면 간장의 상태가 나쁜 사람이 복식호흡을 계속해가면 그 나쁜 상태가 없어져 간장의 검사치가 점점 정상치로 회복되는 것과 같은 현상을 나타내는 일도 있게 되는데 이것도 이상한 일은 아니다. 호흡을 매개로 해서 수의 신경과 부수의 신경 사이를 컨트롤할 수 있다고 하는 하나의 돌파구를 발견할 수 있다고 생각해도 좋을 것이다. 그와 같은 생각은 옛날부터 있어 좌선이라든가 명상법이 동양 고대의 인간을 단련하는 수행법으로 발달해온 것이다.

좌선이나 명상도 숨을 길게 내쉬는 단전호흡법을 기본으로 하고 있어서 원리는 같은 것이다. 최근 여러 기회에 좌선이나 명상을 하고 있을 때의 뇌파가 추정되어 있어 눈을 뜨고 의식이 분명할 때에는 나올 리가 없다고 생각되는 a파도 확인되고 있다. 눈을 뜨고 의식이 명확할 때 통상의 뇌파는 b파인 것이다.

본래 의식으로 어쩔 수 없다고 여겨왔던 대뇌까지 어느 정도 컨트롤할 수 있다는 사실이 서양과학에 의해서 증명되어 있는 것으로 여기서도 정신과 육체를 동시에 컨트롤하는 돌파구가 열리고 있는 것이다. 또 한 가지 복식호흡이 다른 장기를 컨트롤하고 있다고 여겨지는 확실한 증거를 들어본다. 라마즈법이라고 부르는 출산법이 있다는 것을 알고 있으리라 생각되지만 이것도 기본은 복식호흡을 훈련하여 무통 출산으로 이끌고 있다. 그 이유는 복식호흡에 의해서 정신적으로 릴랙스 해지는 결과, 근육이 이완되고 자궁이 부드러워지며 또 복식호흡으로 몸이 긴장 상태에서 개방되면 말초신경의 활동이 개방되면 말초신경의 활동이 억제되어 아픔에 대해 민감하지 않기 때문이다.

복식호흡은 직접적으로는 횡격막의 긴장을 풀고 완전히 뻗어 있어 상하 운동이 뜻대로 안 되는 상태를 릴랙스하게 시켜서 운동하기 쉽게 해주는 것이다. 스트레스가 커져 긴장되면 횡격막은 그다지 움직이지 않게 된다. 긴장하면 어깨와 목 등의 근육이 팽팽해진다. 그렇게 되면 공기가 들어간 채로 있게 되고 나가지 않는다. 나가지 않으면 새 공기가 들어오기 어렵게 되는 것이다.

그래서 긴장을 늦춘다는 말이 중요한 의미를 갖게 된다. 웃거나 노래하거나 하면 긴장이 늦춰진다. 코미디언은 손님을 어떻게 하여 웃길지 고심하는데 그것은 어떻게 긴장을 늦춰 주느냐 하는 것과 같은 것이다. 횡격막이 완전히 뻗어 올라간 것을 어떻게 밀어주는 것이다.

이야기에 집중 긴장시켜 다음에는 웃겨서 긴장을 늦추고 단번에 공기를 내보내 주는 것이다. 긴장시켜 공기를 넣고 웃겨서 공기를 빼준다. 그것을 여러 번 되풀이하면 손님들은 마지막에는 충분히 릴랙스하게 되어 만족하여 돌아간다고 하는 식이다. 손님 측에서는 즐기면서 복식호흡을 만족스럽게 하게 된다.

단전 호흡 및 복식 호흡에 관해선 더 설명을 생략하기로 한다. 호흡훈련을 계속하면 질병을 몰아내고 건강한 몸과 마음을 유지할 수 있음을 믿고 꾸준히 수행에 정진하기 바란다.

MOO YEA DO

수기
(손과 팔의 기술)

수기란 말함은 찌르고 치고 막는 것을 말한다. 무예도는 이어지
(원심)는 공격을 중요시하고 있으므로 모든 기술을 복합적으로 설명
하겠다. 예를 들면 수도로 막고 주먹으로 찌르고 주먹으로 막고 관
수로 찌르고 하여 여러 가지의 공격, 방어를 할 수 있게 손에 변화를
갖는 연습을 일관되게 해야 한다.

주먹 지르기

하나, 대련자세에서 앞에 손으로 수도 방어 오른 주먹 지른다.
둘,　 자세를 바꿔 가며 반복 연습한다.

수도치기

하나, 대련자세에서 앞에 손으로 상단 방어 오른 수도로 목을 친다.
둘,   자세를 바꿔 가며 반복 연습한다.

누르고 지르기

하나, 대련자세에서 앞 손바닥으로 상대의 팔을 누르고 오른 주먹
      지른다.
둘,   자세를 바꿔 가며 반복 연습한다.

망치 주먹치기

하나, 대련자세에서 앞 손으로 방어 혹은 누르고 잡은 후 동시에
      오른손 망치 주먹으로 내려친다.
둘, 자세를 바꿔 가며 반복 연습한다.

등주먹(Back Fist) 치기

하나, 대련자세에서 앞 손으로(장권) 눌러 방어 후 등주먹으로 치기. / 자세를 바꿔 가며 반복 연습한다.

둘, 대련자세에서 앞 수도로 방어 후 같은 손으로 밀친다. / 친다. / 오른손 장권으로 민다. / 친다. / 자세를 바꿔 가며 반복 연습한다.

관수 찌르기

하나, 대련자세에서 양 관수에서 좌 관수 방어, 우관수로 찌른다.

둘, 자세를 바꿔 우관수 방어, 좌 관수로 찌른다.

돌려막기

하나, 대련자세에서 뒷 수도로 왼쪽 팔꿈치 밑으로 돌려막고 왼발이 좌로 일 보 전진하면서 안쪽 수도로 적의 목을 가격한다.

둘,　자세를 바꿔 가며 반복 연습한다.

손끝 찍기

하나, 대련자세에서 앞 손목으로 방어 후 손끝으로 찍어 공격 / 뒷
　　　손 장권으로 얼굴 공격한다.
둘,　자세를 바꿔 가며 반복 연습한다.

밀어던지기

하나, 대련자세에서 왼쪽 수도 방어와 동시 오른발 반보 전진하면
　　　서 양손으로 밀어 던진다.
둘,　자세를 바꿔 가며 반복 연습한다.

수도 되돌려 치기

하나, 상대가 앞 자세 팔꿈치로 밀 때 앞발을 뒤쪽으로 빼면서 중

심을 잃게 한 후 밀린 팔을 수도로 되돌려 친다. 칠 때 왼발
은 상대의 대퇴부에 건다.

관수 찌르기

하나, 대련자세에서 손목을 잡아 아래로 누르면서 다른 관수로 상
　　대를 공격한다.

대련자세에서 상대가 오른발을 앞으로 내디디면서 오른 주먹으로 중단 공격해올 때

하나, 왼손 수도 방어와 동시 왼발을 한 발 뒤로 빼면서 오른발을 상
　　대 오른쪽 대퇴부에 걸고 동시에 오른쪽 역 수도로 상대의 목
　　을 걸어 왼쪽으로 돌릴 때 왼발을 반대 방향 180도 회전한다.

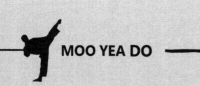 MOO YEA DO

무예도 기본 방어

기본 방어

○ 하단 방어

○ 상단 방어

○ 중단 옆 방어

○ 중단 안 방어

기본 방어 연습에는 동작이 1-5 그리고 반대쪽 연습은 6-10으로 한다.

하단 방어

하나, 준비자세에서 왼발을 오른발 옆으로 모으고 동시에 오른 주
　　　먹은 낭심을 방어하고 왼 주먹은 오른쪽 목을 방어한다. 이
　　　때 숨을 모은다.

둘,　왼발이 앞으로 나가 전굴자세가 되면서 왼팔은 가슴을 스치
　　　면서 아래로 내려 왼쪽 다리 바깥쪽에서 멈춘다. 이때 오른
　　　주먹은 오른쪽 옆구리에 가져가면서 호흡을 토해낸다.

셋,　오른 주먹 중단 공격과 동시에 왼 주먹은 왼쪽 옆구리에 가져
　　　가며 기합을 넣는다.

넷,　왼발을 끌어 오른발에 붙이며 두 주먹을 가슴 앞쪽에 안 주
　　　먹을 위로 모으며 이때 숨을 모은다.

다섯, 왼발을 왼쪽 어깨너비로 벌려 준비자세가 되고 두 주먹을 동
　　　시에 단전 밑으로 힘 있게 내리며 호흡을 입으로 토해낸다.

여섯, 준비자세에서 오른발을 끌어 왼발에 모으고 왼 주먹이 낭심
　　　을 방어하고 오른 주먹은 왼쪽 목을 방어한다. 이때 숨을 모
　　　은다.

일곱, 오른발이 앞으로 나가 전굴자세가 되면서 오른팔이 가슴을
　　　스치면서 아래로 뻗어 오른쪽 다리 옆에서 멈춘다. 동시에 왼

주먹은 왼쪽 옆구리로 가져가며 숨을 토해낸다.

여덟, 왼 주먹으로 중단 지르기를 하며 동시에 오른 주먹은 오른쪽 옆구리로 가져가며 기합을 넣는다.

아홉, 오른발을 끌어 왼발 옆에 붙이고 두 주먹을 가슴 앞쪽에 붙이며 이때 안 주먹은 위로 보게 하며 숨을 모은다.

열,　오른발을 어깨너비로 벌려 준비자세가 되고 두 주먹을 동시에 단전 밑으로 힘 있게 내리며 호흡을 토해낸다.

하단 방어 연습 방법

기본연습 때는 준비자세에서 하나에 왼발을 오른쪽 발에 붙임과 동시에 왼 주먹을 오른쪽 목을 방어한다. 둘에는 왼발을 앞으로 내디디며 전굴자세를 만듦과 동시에 왼팔을 아래로 주먹이 낭심 하단 방어를 하며 셋에는 오른 주먹을 중단 지르기를 하며 기합을 넣는다. 넷에 왼발을 뒤로 빼 오른발에 붙임과 동시에 양 주먹을 가슴 앞으로 모으며 이때 숨을 모은다. 다섯에 왼발을 옆으로 벌림과 동시 양 주먹을 힘 있게 내리면서 단전에 모으고 이때 호흡을 입으로 토해낸다. 반대 방향 연습은 여섯부터 열까지 반복 연습한다(상단 방어. 중단 옆 방어. 중단 안 방어 동일하다).

상단 방어(High Block)

하나, 준비자세에서 왼발을 오른발 옆에 모으고 오른팔을 중단 높
　　　이로 들어 앞으로 내밀고 왼 주먹을 오른쪽 겨드랑이 밑에 댄
　　　다. 이때 주먹 안쪽이 위로 향하게 하고 숨을 모은다.

둘,　왼발이 앞으로 나가 전굴자세가 되고 왼팔은 몸통과 얼굴을
　　　스치듯이 위로 치켜올려 방어 이때 주먹이 팔꿈치보다 약 15
　　　도 각도 위로 올라가야 하며 동시에 오른 주먹은 오른쪽 옆구
　　　리에 가져가며 호흡을 토해낸다.

셋,　왼 주먹을 왼쪽 옆구리로 끌어당기며 동시에 오른 주먹으로
　　　상단 공격하며 기합을 넣는다.

넷,　왼발을 끌어 오른발 옆으로 붙이며 두 주먹을 가슴 앞쪽에
　　　안 주먹은 위를 향하고 숨을 모은다.

다섯, 왼발을 왼쪽 어깨너비로 벌려 준비자세가 되고 두 주먹을 단
　　　전 밑으로 힘 있게 내리며 호흡을 토해낸다.

여섯, 오른발을 왼발에 모으고 왼팔을 중단 높이로 들어 앞으로 내
　　　밀고 오른 주먹을 왼쪽 겨드랑이 밑에 댄다. 이때 주먹 안쪽
　　　이 위로 향하게 하고 숨을 모은다.

일곱, 오른발이 앞으로 나가 전굴자세가 되고 오른팔은 몸통과 얼

굴을 스쳐 위로 치켜올려 방어 이때 주먹이 팔꿈치보다 약 15
도 위로 올라가야 하며 동시에 왼 주먹은 왼쪽 옆구리에 가져
가며 숨을 토해낸다.

여덟, 오른 주먹을 오른쪽 옆구리로 끌어당기며 왼 주먹을 상단 공
격하며 기합을 넣는다.

아홉, 오른발을 끌어 왼발 옆으로 붙이며 두 주먹을 가슴 앞쪽에
안 주먹이 위로 향하게 하고 숨을 모은다.

열, 　오른발을 어깨너비로 벌려 준비자세가 되고 두 주먹을 단전
밑으로 힘 있게 내리며 호흡을 토해낸다.

상단 방어 연습 방법

하단 방어 연습 때와 같은 순서로 방어 동작만 상단으로 하면 된
다. 왼 주먹을 오른쪽 겨드랑이에 붙일 때 주먹 안쪽이 위로 보게 하
며 숨을 들이쉰다. 둘에는 왼발이 앞으로 나가 전굴자세가 되고 왼팔
은 몸통과 얼굴을 스쳐 위로 치켜올려 방어하며 이때 주먹이 팔꿈치
보다 약 15도 각도 위로 올라가야 하며 이때 오른 주먹은 오른쪽 옆
구리에 가져간다. 셋에는 왼 주먹을 왼쪽 옆구리로 끌어당기며 오른
주먹을 상단 공격하며 기합을 넣는다. 넷, 다섯은 하단 방어 때와 동

일하다.

중단 옆 방어(Middle out Side Block)

하나, 준비자세에서 왼발을 오른발에 모으고 오른팔을 중단 높이
　　　로 들고 왼 주먹을 오른팔 겨드랑이 밑에 댄다. 이때 왼 주먹
　　　안쪽이 아래로 향한다. 호흡을 모은다.

둘,　왼발이 앞으로 나가 전굴자세가 되고 왼팔을 45도 각도로 단
　　　전(배꼽) 위 턱 아래로 스치며 왼쪽으로 옆 방어 이때 주먹은
　　　왼쪽 귀와 일직선이어야 하고 오른 주먹은 오른쪽에 가져간
　　　다. 이때 호흡을 토해낸다.

셋,　왼 주먹을 왼쪽 옆구리로 끌어당기며 오른 주먹으로 중단공
　　　격을 하고 기합을 넣는다.

넷,　왼발을 끌어 오른발 옆으로 붙이며 두 주먹을 가슴 앞쪽에
　　　안쪽 주먹이 위로 향하게 하고 숨을 모은다.

다섯, 왼발을 왼쪽 넓이로 벌려 준비자세가 되고 두 주먹을 단전 아
　　　래로 힘 있게 내린다. 호흡을 토해낸다.

여섯, 오른발을 왼발에 모으고 왼팔을 중단 높이로 들고 오른 주먹

을 왼팔 겨드랑이 밑에 댄다. 이때 오른 주먹 안쪽이 아래로 향한다. 호흡을 모은다.

일곱, 오른발이 앞으로 나가 전굴자세가 되고 오른팔을 45도 각도로 단전 위 턱 아래를 스치며 오른쪽으로 방어. 이때 주먹은 오른쪽 귀와 일직선이어야 하고 왼 주먹은 왼쪽 옆구리로 가져간다. 이때 호흡을 토해낸다.

여덟, 오른 주먹을 오른쪽 옆구리로 끌어당기며 왼 주먹으로 중단 공격하며 기합을 넣는다.

아홉, 오른발을 끌어 왼발 옆으로 붙이며 두 주먹을 가슴 앞쪽에, 안 주먹이 위로 향하게 하고 숨을 모은다.

열, 오른발을 오른쪽 어깨너비로 벌려 준비자세가 되고 두 주먹을 동시에 단전 앞으로 힘 있게 내리며 호흡을 토해낸다. 이때 두 주먹은 단전과 주먹 하나 간격이어야 한다.

중단 옆 방어 연습 방법

하나, 준비자세에서 왼발을 오른발에 모으고 오른팔을 중단 높이로 들고 왼 주먹을 오른팔 겨드랑이 밑에 댄다. 이때 왼 주먹 안쪽이 아래로 향한다. 이때 호흡을 모은다.

둘, 왼발이 앞으로 나가 전굴자세가 되고 왼팔을 45도 각도로 단
    전 위 턱 아래로 스치며 왼쪽으로 방어, 이때 주먹은 왼쪽 귀
    와 일직선이어야 하고 오른쪽 주먹은 옆구리에 가져가며 이때
    호흡을 토해낸다.

셋, 왼 주먹을 옆구리로 끌어당기며 오른 주먹으로 중단 공격하
    며 기합을 넣는다.

넷, 왼발을 끌어 오른발 옆으로 붙이며 두 주먹을 가슴 앞쪽에
    안 주먹이 위쪽을 향하게 하고 숨을 모은다.

다섯, 왼발을 왼쪽 어깨너비로 벌려 준비자세가 되고 두 주먹을 단
    전 앞으로 힘 있게 내리며 호흡을 토해낸다.

중단 안 방어(Inside Middle Block)

하나, 준비자세에서 왼발을 오른발 옆으로 모으고 오른팔을 중단
    으로 내밀고 왼 주먹을 왼쪽 귀 옆으로 가져간다. 이때 주먹
    안쪽이 앞으로 향하고 숨을 모은다.

둘, 왼발이 앞으로 나가 전굴자세가 되고 왼 주먹을 턱 높이로 왼
    쪽 귀 옆에서 오른쪽 귀 앞으로 방어와 동시에 오른 주먹은
    오른쪽 옆구리로 가져가며 호흡을 토해낸다.

셋, 왼 주먹을 왼쪽 옆구리로 끌어당기며 동시에 오른 주먹으로 중단 공격하며 기합을 넣는다.

넷, 왼발을 끌어 오른발 옆에 붙이며 두 주먹을 가슴 앞쪽에, 이때 안 주먹이 위로 향하게 하고 호흡을 모은다.

다섯, 왼발을 어깨너비로 벌려 준비자세가 되고 두 주먹을 단전 앞으로 힘 있게 내리며 이때 주먹과 단전 사이는 주먹 하나의 공간이어야 하고 숨을 토해낸다.

여섯, 오른발을 왼발 옆에 모으고 왼팔을 중단으로 내밀고 오른 주먹을 오른쪽 귀 옆에 가져간다. 이때 주먹 안쪽이 앞으로 향하여 숨을 모은다.

일곱, 오른발이 앞으로 나가 전굴자세가 되고 오른 주먹을 턱 높이로 오른쪽 귀 옆에서 왼쪽 귀 앞으로 방어, 왼 주먹은 왼쪽 옆구리로 가져가며 호흡을 토해낸다.

여덟, 오른 주먹을 오른쪽 옆구리에 끌어당기며 동시에 왼 주먹으로 중단 공격하며 기합을 넣는다.

아홉, 오른발을 끌어 왼발 옆에 붙이며 두 주먹을 가슴 앞쪽에, 이때 안 주먹은 위로 향하게 하고 호흡을 모은다.

열, 오른발을 어깨너비로 벌려 준비자세가 되고 두 주먹을 단전 앞으로 힘 있게 내리며 동시에 호흡을 토해낸다.

MOO YEA DO

족기
(기본 발차기)

족기

○ **앞차기**

○ **돌려차기**

○ **옆차기**

○ **회전차기**

○ **뒤차기**

앞 다리 올리기

준비자세(왼쪽)

하나, 바닥을 스치는 점프를 하면서 오른 다리를 뒤로하는 전굴자
세가 된다. 이때 두 팔은 엑스자로 상단 방어를 하며 전굴자세

가 됨과 동시 좌우 양옆으로 뻗어내린다(어깨에서 아래로 45도).

둘, 오른 다리를 오른쪽 귀 옆으로 뻗어 올리고 내릴 때 양팔은
엑스자로 상단 방어하며 전굴자세가 됨과 동시에 좌우 양옆
으로 뻗어 내린다(어깨 아래로 45도).

   * 자세(오른쪽)를 바꿔 연습

안다리 후리기

준비자세(왼쪽)

하나, 다리 올리기 준비자세와 동일

둘, 왼팔을 뻗어 앞으로 내민다.

셋, 오른쪽 다리를 들어 안으로 후려 왼쪽 손바닥을 때린다(오른
손은 오른쪽 옆구리에 댄다).

넷, 오른쪽 다리를 반대 방향으로 원위치에 돌아온다.

   * 자세(오른쪽)를 바꿔 연습

밖으로 후리기

준비자세(왼쪽)

하나, 안다리 후리기와 동일

둘, 오른 다리를 들어 왼쪽 어깨부터 가슴 위 얼굴을 스쳐 크게 반원을 그리며 원위치로 돌아온다. 양팔은 엑스자로 상단 방어하며 전굴자세가 됨과 동시에 좌우 양옆으로 뻗어 내린다 (어깨 아래로 45도).

앞차기

대련자세(왼쪽)

하나, 양쪽 발을 45도 왼쪽으로 틀고 몸통이 정면으로 향하게 한다.

둘, 오른 무릎을 45도 각도로 쳐든다.

셋, 쳐든 무릎을 힘차게 목표에 타격한다(이때 발가락은 뒤로 제치고 앞발 안쪽으로 가격한다).

넷, 가격한 발이 원위치로 돌아온다.

　 * 오른쪽 자세로 바꾸어 같은 방법으로 연습한다

돌려 차기

대련자세(왼쪽)

하나, 오른발을 (무릎) 들고 동시에 왼발을 45도 정도 몸통을 왼쪽
    으로 튼다.

둘,   오른쪽 발등으로 목표물을 타격, 동시에 왼쪽 발바닥 앞쪽으
    로 몸통을 튼다.

셋,   오른발은 원위치로 돌아온다.

    *오른쪽 자세로 바꾸어 같은 방법으로 연습한다

옆차기

대련자세(왼쪽)

하나, 오른쪽 무릎을 90도로 꺾어 완전히 명치 가까이 올리고
    왼발을 틀어 몸통을 오른쪽 어깨가 목표물을 향하게 하며
    이때 오른팔은 90도로 꺾어 단전 위 명치를 방어하고 왼쪽
    주먹은 왼쪽 옆구리에 가져간다. 이때 주먹 안쪽이 위로 향
    한다.

둘, 쳐든 무릎을 뻗어 목표물을 타격(발의 옆 부위 뒤축), 동시에 왼쪽 발을 왼쪽으로 틀어주므로 타격이 강해진다.

셋, 반대 방향(오른쪽)으로 몸통을 돌림과 동시에 오른발이 원위치로 돌아온다.

* 오른쪽 자세로 바꿔 연습한다.

회전차기

대련자세(왼쪽)

하나, 오른쪽 다리를 안 후리기 한 후 왼발 옆에 놓음과 동시에 왼발이 왼쪽 방향으로 360도 회전 하여 대련자세가 된다.

둘, 안다리 후리기는 상대 주먹, 발 공격을 방어하며 또는 상단을 공격한다.

셋, 회전하는 발은 상대의 상단, 즉 머리 부위를 공격한다(앞 발바닥, 뒤축을 사용한다).

* 자세를 바꾸어 계속 연습한다.

뒤차기

대련자세(왼쪽)

하나, 오른쪽으로 상체를 돌려 목표물을 응시하고 오른발을 끌어
     왼발 옆에 모으고 이때 무릎을 굽히며 오른팔을 오른쪽 옆구
     리에, 왼팔을 들어 왼손으로 왼쪽 옆얼굴 부위를 방어한다.

둘,   오른쪽 무릎을 듦과 동시에 뒤축으로 목표물을 타격한다. 이
     때 오른팔은 발차기와 반대 방향으로 뻗는다.

셋,   오른발을 반대 방향으로 회전하여 대련 자세가 된다. 시선은
     항상 정면을 응시한다.

   * 자세(오른쪽)를 바꿔 같은 순서대로 반복 연습한다.

하나부터 열까지 자기방어(Basic Self Defence)

상대가 양손으로 양쪽 어깨를 잡았을 때

하나, 양팔을 엑스자로 가슴 앞에 모은다. 이때 손 안쪽이 가슴을
　　　 향하게 한다.

둘,　 양팔을 45도 각도로 위로 해쳐 올린다. 이때 손바닥이 상대
　　　 를 향한다.

셋,　 양손을 끌어 양 가슴에 모은다. 손바닥이 상대를 향한다.

넷,　 왼발이 앞으로 나가 전굴자세가 되며 양손(장권)으로 상대 가
　　　 슴 부위를 세차게 가격한다.

상대가 양손으로 양쪽 어깨를 잡았을 때

하나, 양팔을 상대 머리 위 높이로 쳐든다. 양 손바닥은 자기를 향
　　　한다.
둘,　양수도로 상대가 잡은 왼쪽 팔꿈치를 세차게 액스자로 아래
　　　로 내려치며 이때 양수도는 양 어깨너비로 벌리고 오른쪽 다
　　　리는 일 보 후퇴하며 전굴자세가 된다.
셋,　뒤로 뺀 발로 상대를 가격한다(앞차기).

상대가 양손으로 양쪽 어깨를 잡았을 때

하나, 왼손을 왼쪽 귀 옆으로 올리며 동시에 왼발을 좌로 벌려 기마
　　　자세가 되며 왼팔 앞쪽으로 상대 오른쪽 팔꿈치를 우측으로
　　　치면서 동시에 상체를 우측으로 튼다.
둘,　왼손으로 상대 오른쪽 어깨를 잡으며 오른팔 역 수도로 상대
　　　의 왼쪽 목을 걸어 오른발이 왼쪽으로 회전과 동시에 상대의
　　　오른쪽 옆다리를 걸고 왼쪽으로 밀어 던진다.

하나, 오른손을 오른쪽 귀 옆으로 올리며 동시에 오른발을 우로 벌
　　　려 기마자세가 되며 오른팔 앞쪽으로 상대 왼쪽 팔꿈치를 왼
　　　쪽으로 튼다.

둘,　오른손으로 상대 오른쪽 어깨를 잡으며 왼팔 역 수도로 상대
　　　의 오른쪽 목을 걸어 왼발이 오른쪽으로 회전과 동시에 상대
　　　의 왼쪽 옆다리를 걸고 오른쪽으로 밀어 던진다.

상대가 양손으로 양쪽 어깨를 잡았을 때

하나, 왼팔을 들어 상대 오른팔 안 팔꿈치를 수도(손바닥이 자기를 향
　　　함)로 내리침과 동시에 오른 손바닥으로 상대 왼쪽 팔꿈치를 밀
　　　쳐 올린다. 이때 왼쪽 발은 왼쪽으로 일 보 후퇴.

둘,　왼손으로 상대 오른 팔꿈치를 잡으며 오른발을 왼쪽으로 일
　　　보 전진(상대 오른쪽 옆다리) 회전하며 상대 오른팔을 끌어당기
　　　고 상대 왼쪽 팔꿈치를 상대 오른쪽으로 밀쳐 던진다.

하나, 오른팔을 들어 상대 왼팔 안 팔꿈치를 수도(손바닥이 자기를 향
　　　함)로 내려침과 동시에 왼손바닥으로 상대 오른쪽 팔꿈치를
　　　밀쳐 올린다. 이때 오른쪽 발은 오른쪽으로 일 보 후퇴.

둘, 　오른손으로 상대 왼쪽 팔꿈치를 잡으며 왼발을 오른쪽으로
　　　일 보 전진(상대 왼쪽 옆다리) 회전하며 상대 왼팔을 끌어당기며
　　　상대 오른쪽 팔꿈치를 상대 왼쪽으로 밀쳐 던진다.

상대가 양손으로 양쪽 어깨를 잡았을 때

하나, 오른팔을 들어 상대 오른쪽 손날을 잡고 왼손을 아래로 상대
　　　의 왼쪽 손목을 잡는다.

둘, 　왼발을 좌 옆으로 내디딤과 동시에 몸을 오른쪽으로 회전하
　　　면서 왼팔을 당겨 상대 오른팔 팔꿈치에 걸어 상대 팔꿈치를
　　　직각으로 세워 상대 왼쪽으로 밈과 동시에 상대 왼쪽 손목을
　　　아래로 잡아당긴다.

셋, 　왼팔을 들어 상대 왼쪽 손날을 잡고 오른손은 아래로 상대의
　　　오른 손목을 잡는다.

넷, 오른발이 오른쪽으로 내디딤과 동시 몸을 왼쪽으로 회전하면서 오른팔을 당겨 상대 왼쪽 팔꿈치에 걸어 상대 팔꿈치를 직각으로 세워 상대 오른쪽으로 밈과 동시 상대 오른 손목을 아래로 잡아당긴다.

MOO YEA DO

MOO YEA DO

- The Way of Discipline Art

Who is World Grandmaster Tiger Yang?

Grand Master Tiger Yang is a brilliant exponent of the Martial Arts on the American scene. Tiger has appeared in 8 films produced in Hong Kong by Golden Harvest. Mr. Yang, also a Martial Arts Director, has proven to be one of the Southeast Asia's most popular Kung Fu stars since early 1975-1980- making a total of 30 films. He has now started a new Hollywood film, "Devil's Gambit", as starring role produced by United Cinema Feature and "Operation Overkill" produced by Cinema Features Inc., 1982. Others include "Mission Killfast" 1991, "Omega Assassins" 1992, "Death Penalty" 1994, the International AB Flex Commercial and more. He has showed his great strength on *The Tonight Show starring Johnny Carson*, and he has made frequent appearances on local stations in the Chicago area. On British Television he demonstrated his most spectacular exploit- pulling a truck carrying 50 people with his teeth. The combined weight exceeded 6 tons. Tiger has duplicated this show of power and will on numerous occasions, one in the USA. Also with his teeth, he can lift a 200 pound barbell from the floor to full standing position and then walk with the weight.

Tiger Yang speaks five languages – Cantonese, Mandarin, Korean, English, and Vietnamese.

When it was suggested to Muhammad Ali that he could benefit from the discipline of Tae Kwon Do, one of the Marital Arts, Tiger Yang was chose as coach and instructor – champion to champion. Tiger traveled with Ali to Germany, Jamaica, The Philippines, Korea and was with him in Japan during the famous Ali-Jnoki fight in 1976.

Tiger is lightsome six foot man who has been exercising Tae Kwon Do since childhood. He was proclaimed World Champion of the Heavyweight Division at the World Tae Kwon Do Tournament in Japan in 1969 and 1971.

Over the years, Tiger has developed his highly personal version of Moo Yea-Do which has become known in Martial Arts circles as the *Tiger Style*. It combines fierceness with the extraordinary beauty, power and spirit of Tae Kwon Do, Kung Fu and Karate. The *Tiger Style* is so uniquely Tiger's own that is has become his signature.

Tiger, who is one of the only twenty people in the world to hold a 9th Rank of Tae Kwon Do and who holds a 10th degree Black Belt in Moo Yea-Do, taught at the Vietnam Military College. He has conducted classes for members of the United States 8th Division stationed in Korea and has taught CIA agents in Washington D.C., as well as at the Chicago III. Police Academy. He is now the founder of Moo Yea-Do to which he holds a 10th Degree Black Belt. Currently he is the President of the International Moo Yea-Do Federation, President of the World Tae Kwon Do Master's Union and President of the Martial Arts Film Actor's Association. In 2017, World Grandmaster Tiger Yang was honored with a place in the Hall of Fame for his achievements, and in 2020, The U.S. Tae Kwon Do Grandmasters Society selected Grand Master Tiger Yang to receive the 2020 Hall of Fame "Grandmaster of the Year" award.

What is Moo Yea-Do?

The study of the martial arts is the study of truth based on natural movements that have been developed down through the ages. Created out of conflict, necessity and the human experience, studying martial arts reveals constant truths. Even as particular methods and expressions change and evolve to adapt to new circumstances, the underlying principles stay the same. The martial arts that have been taught for years promote a basic principle: through discipline and training a true martial artist will continuously be an example of true humanity, someone who realizes and who promotes in others the understanding that it is more honorable and important to help create an orderly and harmonious society than just to develop fighting skills.

Moo Yea-Do is a new form of martial art that I created in 1980. It is a combination of many different martial arts that have been passed down from generation to generation; including Tae Kwon Do, Kung Fu, and Hap Ki Do. I mastered these martial arts through more than 29 years of training. I studied Tae Kwon Do up to 9th Dan black belt, and I learned Kung Fu and Hap Ki Do from my work in 23 Chinese martial arts movies. Taking the best parts from each of these martial arts, I put them together in a way most suited to today's society. My hope is that mental and physical training based on Moo Yea-Do will help people all over the world to join in creating healthier and more peaceful, orderly societies.

Studying basic but unique movements will combine both mental and physical abilities while training. Besides keeping your body healthy, you will discover that one of the most valuable aspects of your training is that you will be able to use this knowledge in your life to keep your mind peaceful. Of course, I must let you know that you cannot master a martial art overnight. It takes time. But repetition -- practicing over and over again -- is how you will obtain the true value of the martial art. I can assure you that there are no geniuses when it comes to learning a martial art; only through training will you be able to master it. I hope this book will become a big part of your life and be helpful through your journey.

1. What is Moo Yea-Do's particular theory?

No matter what it is, in order to understand and become accustomed to something, you need to grasp its specific underlying theory. Moo Yea-Do's distinguishing theory focuses on movement of the mind. Mind movement is the power to move naturally that comes from one's mentality. A single movement of the mind can make all the body parts move, and that is the theory of Moo Yea-Do. All movements within Moo Yea-Do come from the mind through adaptation to a natural flow of energy. Therefore, Moo Yea-Do's movement of the mind is based on awareness of the universe itself. Moo Yea-Do's theory is based on the truth of the universe as the root of mental movement, and its application to the adaptation of training is the path to a profound discipline in today's society. The reason why Moo Yea-Do is based on mind movement is that one gets the power to know an opponent's movement only by first gaining the power to acknowledge the order of the universe expressed in the movement of all living things, and specifically through the movement of the human mind and body. Through Moo Yea-Do training you will learn the technique of moving your mind in order to most effectively move your body.

2. Harmony of Moo Yea-Do(Bond)

Moo Yea-Do's mental movement is based on the combination

of the mind and the body. Mental movement is transformed into physical movement. Therefore, movement that comes from the mind can be controlled with respect to the level of power used. For example, when you throw your fist to gain ascendancy over an opponent, you can control how hard you want the impact to be within that short distance before you actually touch his body. Developing that mind control is the type of training that you will need in order to get rid of the mental and physical stresses of today's society. You can clear your mind through the flow of energy, and use that energy to build a stronger body and keep your body from aging, and also to help your blood flow more smoothly so your body stays healthy.

3. Making concentration stronger through mind movement

In Moo Yea-Do, when all the movements occur at a close distance and you must be ready to change your movements as soon as you hit something, you will need to practice so you can use your mind to evaluate your opponent's strength and recognize his technique. But we also need to practice our morals in our daily lives in order to acknowledge and respect others. Moo Yea-Do training is a perfect way to practice our morality. It is not easy to understand everything that occurs, but continuous training will help make it possible.

When you show your true strength over one hundred times, you will develop the kind of strength that is hard to imagine. For example, when a little child gets caught under the tires of a vehicle, a mother will lift that vehicle without thinking and without even breaking a sweat to save her baby -- an amazing situation. But when strength from the mind and the body combine, a type of concentration will form like no other. No matter who you are, if you study and practice the mind movement from Moo Yea-Do, you can always summon extraordinary strength from your mind.

Why is Moo Yea-Do Needed by Modern Society?

If Moo Yea-Do was like any other martial art from the old days, where the only reason for its existence was to build your strength and to learn to fight to protect the honor of your name, then it would not be needed by today's society. But in today's society, we are in need of a sport to give you a healthy body and to keep your mind clear in daily life. That is what Moo Yea-Do does. It is important to keep up with modern customs and to follow the right path not just to practice the simple techniques of the martial arts, but to practice what is needed to benefit the entire human race.

Moo Yea-Do is distinct and different from other martial arts, and is not presented in the old-fashioned way. The substance of Moo Yea-Do embodies respect, responsibility, and honor. It is also based on a healthy mind, a healthy body, and honesty and integrity. The training develops all these qualities, and that is what sets Moo Yea-Do apart from all other martial arts. This is the reason why Moo Yea-Do is profoundly necessary for our modern society.

To gain the full value from training, you will need to have a solid foundation from which you can development of the techniques that are most useful in today's society. As mentioned earlier, Moo Yea-Do is based on Tae Kwon Do, Kwang Po, and Hop Ki Do, which were passed down from generation to generation, combined with a selection of diverse techniques that are the most useful and effective. When you train with the techniques from the martial arts, the training focuses your mind and allows you to be centered and in unison with your body. You must learn how to unite the body, the "heart," and the mind so you can harness all of your strength.

In Moo Yea-Do, strength is most important -- you always need to be able to instantly pour out your strength. You will be able to pour out unlimited power when you learn that the source of strength is making human nature be at one with the universe.

Life of Moo Yea-Do

As the creator of Moo Yea-Do, I hope that through Moo Yea-Do, people all over the world will live in harmony with love and have a healthy life. This is the primary teaching of Moo Yea-Do: becoming one with the universe through training one's mind and body (the small universe) creates harmony. Every movement that occurs based on the natural order of things will be unified and there will be no conflict; each movement will be in harmony with the others. It is this type of thinking that makes people from all over the world want to learn Moo Yea-Do -- even with its relatively short history – as it spreads from California to different states, and also to other countries. Moo Yea-Do is becoming a part of the regular daily life of many people from different cultures and backgrounds.

The second principle of Moo Yea-Do concerns heart. In Moo Yea-Do, "heart" is the center – the center of your mind and the center of your body. Your body and your mind need to combine and connect in a natural, unhindered manner and form a unity with the larger universe based on these factors: sincerity, bravery, and courtesy.

The third principle of Moo Yea-Do focuses on the body. The

physical training in Moo Yea-Do connects the student with nature (the universe), thereby promoting unity with nature. The movement is strong, yet soft. When the cultivation of movement through natural reflex occurs, it is good for the health and also good for defending yourself.

The combination of these elements in Moo Yea-Do makes it particularly well-suited and beneficial for today's stressful society.

A. Grasping the Concept of Strength in Moo Yea-Do Techniques
(Fundamental Characteristics)

The knowledge you learn from training Moo Yea-Do is impossible to completely analyze and explain in a Western context because it was created in Eastern culture and is based on the essence of the Eastern martial arts. To learn Eastern moral sensibilities, a student must have guidance and receive explanation of the concepts.

I need to explain the concept of strength as the source of power in Moo Yea-Do, and the movements that generate this strength. Through Moo Yea-Do training, you learn to generate and use strength. But no matter what your occupation, you can use the strength developed 10 times more in your daily life than on the training floor.

Everyone has a different way of thinking when it comes to the concept of strength because it depends on context and experience. Strength is often the subject of old texts, and had many different meanings. It could be used as a philosophical term or just as a biological reference. Therefore, instead of approaching the concept intellectually, the student's body should just learn through training.

You can say that nature is the source of strength, just as in the bigger picture it is the source of all human life. In other words, humans absorb the life of the universe – spirit -- into the body by breathing. Through training, you can summon and pour out more spirit. That is the purpose of learning Moo Yea-Do; to discover techniques which are consistent with nature. As the creator of Moo Yea-Do, I emphasize that spirit is Moo Yea-Do. This is simple, yet contains a deeper meaning, as mentioned earlier. When you put the philosophical and the biological meanings of spirit together, you begin to get an idea. To discover your strength and to be able to use it freely, you will need to train rigorously and frequently. But remember that training which just builds strength is wrong, if that strength cannot be used freely. Then what is the right approach to training?

To learn the techniques of Moo Yea-Do, you first need to have a mind that is not distracted by aggression or anxiety. A calm mind and quiet demeanor will naturally make your opponents relax so they are not ready to use their strength. Do not let your opponent's strength worry you.

Secondly, always focus your efforts during training on finding the source of your strength – your "heart" that comes from unifying your mind and body in the center to focus your power. Power is formed from the unique techniques of Moo Yea-Do which allow the spirit, your energy, to move most freely. It is in the freedom of natural movements that a student discovers how to summon strength.

B. Flow of Strength

Everything in nature is filled with energy. The movement of that energy is what we call the flow of strength. The flow of strength means when you show your true strength, it comes out naturally without any binds or limitations. There is a tale that when an average sword fighter ran into his parents' enemy, he closed his eyes and blindly stabbed at his opponent. He won, even though the opponent was a master with the sword. This tale shows that when a person is in a desperate position, the mind can take over one's usual abilities and find and use extraordinary hidden strength to overcome danger and prevail.

A famous swordsman said this: "If it comes to you, take it. If it goes away from you, then let it go. If you are face to face, fight with the passion. Fifty-five is ten (5+5), twenty-eight is ten (2+8), and nineteen is also ten (1+9). Therefore, just go with the flow." This is the way strength flows naturally when using the body. You do not wait for your opponent to come and attack, and then let the opponent go. Rather, make the opponent think that it is better for the opponent to come and attack first. When that happens, then deal with the process. You can reach the high point of this flow by practicing every day.

C. Equality of Energy, Mind, and the Body

The importance of knowing strength, and how hard it is to let one's strength flow freely, has already been discussed. But, when one attempts to release unhindered, extraordinary power using natural energy, and the strength of the mind through the body, while they are disconnected and are all over the place, nothing is achieved.

Without a firm bond between the heart and the mind to focus mental ability in order to make the body move, there can only be an unnatural result. The analogy is a human being who dies instantly if there is a failure of any vital organ.

Since a long time ago, Buddhism has taught that under natural laws, not using one's talent causes actual pain. Moo Yea-Do's purpose is to teach one to practice this unification of the heart (spirit), mind and body. When you can control your opponent as easily as you control a part of yourself through these techniques, then you will be a master; you will be able to summon and unleash virtually unlimited power with heart, mind, and body unified in purpose and execution. You will need to practice the way to release this power no matter where, when, and what kind of situation you are in. This practice needs to become the focus for training Moo Yea-Do.

Standard Forms and Rules of Movement

1. Forms Used in the Training Process

Moo Yea-Do does not have many forms (sequences of movements demonstrating various stances and techniques). For beginners, the emphasis is on practicing a few repeated movements. These are targeted to developing both the upper and lower halves of one's body. One must stabilize the body using both legs, which is the best way to utilize energy. A strong upper body and skilled arms are ineffective if the lower half of the body is weak and unstable. A weak lower body interferes with the natural release of energy, and thus prevents a build up of overall energy and strength.

To attain the black belt level, a student must perfect a total of eight forms, each of which is associated with the color of a student's belt:

    a.   Moo Yea Ill Chang (White)

    b.   Moo Yea E Chang (Yellow)

    c.   Moo Yea Sam Chang (Orange)

    d.   Moo Yea Sa Chang (Purple)

e.   Moo Yea O Chang (Green)

f.   Moo Yea Yuk Chang (Blue)

g.   Moo Yea Chil Chang (Brown)

h.   Moo Yea Pal Chang (Red)

Additionally, the student must come to understand the purpose of training, and to adapt their training to their own particular attributes and talents. Developing mental strength, not just physical strength, is one of the most important aspects to be understood.

Moo Yea-Do's first three forms (white, yellow and orange) emphasize learning the basic two center positions.

The next two forms (purple and green) concentrate on the hip area, resulting in smoother kicks and the development of flexibility and versatility.

The sixth (blue) form uses both hand and leg techniques, and a subsequent inhaling tactic is introduced to sustain energy and strength. This level teaches special attack tactics (left and right), and creative ways to get the opponent.

The seventh and eighth forms (brown and red) employ various poses and movements, designed to confuse and to make the opponent nervous. These forms develop offensive and defensive skills, and enhance the flexibility of the waist. Deep, whole body inhaling techniques are employed, which keenly develop one's focus. These forms combine both the mental and the physical attributes of the student – the internal and the external. Instructors assist each student with both defensive and offensive moves, and teach the overall objectives of Moo Yea-Do training.

Moo Yea-Do's Standard Positions

1. Horse Stance

2. Forward Stance

3. Basic Cat Stance

4. Wide Cat Stance

5. Scissors Stance

6. Standing Position

Moo Yea-Do's standard positions are much the same as the standard positions of other martial arts. These standard positions are important in Moo Yea-Do and have a great effect in gathering and applying strength.

1. Horse Stance

Allow a space between your legs as if you are riding a horse and angle your toes and your knees inward at a 15-degree angle. Stay in a low sitting position and try to act like you are pushing your knees toward the inside (the better to grip the horse). Put your knees slightly forward and put strength in your heels, the back of your knees and your butt. The heels, the butt and the upper body need to form a straight line.

When you are executing a low stance, you need to keep your chin down and exhale your breath strongly and completely. Focus your power by concentrating on breathing, and try to focus your strength in the center – your core.

2. Forward Stance

The forward stance is also called the walking position because of the big forward step you take -- just like walking. Start with your feet as wide apart as your shoulders. Step forward with your right foot, and bend your front knee to a 45 degree angle (your shin straight up and down). 70 percent of the weight needs to transfer to the front foot. The left leg needs to be straight with 30 percent of the weight. The toes of the front foot need to face slightly towards the inside, and the toes of the rear foot need to angle forward. The feet need to stay flat on the ground, and the upper body and the head need to be straight and centered. The purpose of this position is to strengthen the legs, so you need to focus strength in the legs and not twist your waist. This position is necessary to attack and push the opponent.

3. Basic Cat Stance

In this position, you put all the weight on the rear leg, with the knee flexed, and the toes pointed to the side. Put no weight on the front foot, and just lightly put the ball of the foot on the ground six to eight inches from the rear foot, with the foot angled slightly to the inside. This position is like a huddled cat, so it is called the "cat stance."

This position, with all the weight on the rear leg and none on the front, and with a narrow space between the feet, is good for quick movement, especially when backing away. It is also very useful for faster and more effective attacks to the opponent's lower area.

4. Wide Cat Stance

From the basic, narrow cat stance position, step forward with the front foot and angle the toes slightly towards the inside. Keep the back foot facing sideways, and retain sixty percent of the weight on the rear leg. Put 40 percent of the weight on the front leg. In Moo yea-do, this position is known as the wide cat stance. It is used for offense to hit the opponent, and also for defense to intercept when the opponent attacks, and to block and pull the opponent to the side. It is a good position for change. The wide position is good for focusing energy when attacking, and effective for defense.

5. Scissors Stance

To achieve this position, start with the feet slightly apart (8 – 10 inches). Step forward with one leg, and bend the knee as the front foot is turned sideways, with the toes pointing outward (the waist must twist so the opposite shoulder comes forward). Put seventy percent of the weight on the front leg. Lift the heel of the rear foot, with the ball of the foot kept on the ground, and retain thirty percent of the weight on the rear leg. With this position, you can turn left or right, or turn your body front and back to attack and defend. This stance allows attacks against the opponent with many different tactics. You can learn this position through a lot of hard training.

6. Standing Position

This position is the one where you have to stand on only one leg. The leg that is standing has to be flexed at the knee to maintain balance. The other leg must be raised with a quick but smooth movement; the knee comes up so that it is bent and faces to the front, with the foot down toward the ground. Your upper body cannot move around and must remain still. This position used to avoid attacks to the lower area, and to attack the opponent with your feet.

There are more positions besides these, but rather then knowing many different techniques superficially, it is best to train with focus and master one technique. Only the repetition of training is the way to become a master and a true warrior.

Basic Breathing Exercises Control and Supplement Energy

People use different ways to control and conserve their energy. Singing and screaming, even yelling, are helpful for releasing stress. Doing these things makes you breathe harder, and by doing so, you recover your energy. Just lying down anywhere can relieve your tiredness, and useful in rebuilding your strength. There are people who constantly read books to try and learn how to increase their energy and develop strength. Knowledge from books can be helpful, but learning must be combined with continuous practice. Someone who feels a bit off when they miss their regular round of Sunday golf, or someone who practices martial arts regularly and can't go to the gym, feels a loss of energy -- a disconnection from the strength of their body. There are people who go to the sauna to release their sweat and stress, and others who run on a daily basis unconditionally. No particular method is the best. What is important is choosing the method which is the best and most suitable for them. Even more important is that they stick with whatever method they choose. People who have bad blood flow will benefit from running or jogging, which enhances strength and helps the blood flow better. People with too much water can go to a sauna to release that excess water from their body through perspiration, balancing out one's system. Every person's energy level depends on a proper balance of blood and water inside their body. If these aspects become unbalanced, a person will lose energy and will eventually become unhealthy and even sick.

There are ways to get more strength which involve methods to keep the blood healthy, and to keep the water-balance of the body healthy.

A. How to better retain your strength.

Talk a lot to convert your emotions, or practice martial arts with loud yelling, or practice yoga, or even watch a comedy to laugh out loud. Practice your breathing by centering your focus on the breath and the sound.

B. How to keep blood healthy.

Ways to make the blood flow better include running, martial arts, or gymnastics – anything which requires your body to move and exert itself. Also, taking a bath makes your body feel hot and makes your blood flow more smoothly.

C. The way to keep fluids balanced.

Anything that makes you sweat is good. The best way to do this is in the sauna, but even a regular bath can make you sweat, as well as jogging and running. All of these methods will make you feel better.

You need to get away from work mentally and physically to recover strength that has been exhausted. The easiest way is to have a conversation. Even if you don't laugh out loud, just having a good conversation is the best "medicine" for making yourself feel better. Even when you are not feeling good, just by talking for an hour or two, you will experience something that rises up from inside -- a feeling that makes you want to do something. One might think it is a waste of time to form a group and have a conversation, but according to the logic of developing a healthier spirit, it is good to do that. This method will let your spirit pull away from what had been its focus, and allow it focus on something different. Through conversation, the change in focus can redirect attention away from a bad or stressful experience, and unconsciously figure out a way to play, instead.

Another way to supplement spirit in the body is to breathe hard -- in a conscious and positive way. A good way is to practice this repetitious breathing is by jogging or running. Conscious repetitious breathing makes your body accept your spirit getting stronger. As mentioned, there are many ways to practice repetitious breathing. For example, singing naturally requires focused repetitious breathing.

The theory is to push down the diaphragm, and then to pull it back up. Any kind of breathing moves the diaphragm, but the amplitude of the movement is what really matters. The movement of the diaphragm in females may be smaller than that in males, so they may naturally take smaller breaths. But the ability to move the diaphragm feely thorough multiple breaths is the crucial idea.

In repetitious, "multiple" breathing, there are western methods and eastern methods. In the western method, when you let out air, you pull your stomach in, and when you inhale, release your stomach out. These actions make the diaphragm move up and down. You can do this by sitting on a chair or lying down facing up. Through multiple breathing, you can make strength flow throughout the entire body. First, breath in softly and slowly expand your navel area making it round, and then let your breath out slowly and pull your stomach in. It is good to take as much time as you can, and also to push down on your lower belly to release all the air. When you are taking a breath in, a duration of 2-3 seconds is enough, but when you are letting your breath out, you need to continue to let it out for as long as 20-30 seconds. Ideally, the exhalation should last as long as a minute. For best results, one should repeat the process three times every morning, in the afternoon, and at night.

Next is the eastern way of breathing. In contrast to the western way of breathing (where the stomach is pulled in when exhaling, and then released when inhaling), with the eastern method of breathing you exert great pressure on your lower stomach when breathing. Because of that, the amount of air that can be pulled inside the body is greatly increased, so that your body can be even more energized. Here is simple way to practice the method of breathing. Either stand or sit, make your back straight, and exert focused pressure under your belly button. Relax your shoulders, so only the focused area will have strength. Let your upper body fall while slowly and completely breathing out. Start with an exhalation lasting from 2 to 3 seconds, but after getting use to it, work up to breathing out for 30 seconds. After exhaling, raise your upper body while breathing in.

Practice of this eastern multiple breathing method will also discipline the brain stem. The brain stem is the most basic and primitive part of the brain. And if you discipline this area, the animal instinct will get stronger. In other words, it will help develop a part of brain that no one consciously uses. The brain stem has an important connection to your strength. How does this breathing method help discipline the brain stem? A human's nervous system is divided into two types of nerves, the ones which you can move voluntarily, and the ones that you cannot voluntarily control. The involuntary nerves are located near the brain stem that deals with animal instinct. The brain stem controls all of the rhythms of the body, such as sleep, breathing, and the control of internal fluids. The nerve impulses that control internal organs like our heart, liver and lungs continue unconsciously whether we are awake or asleep. These nerve impulses move freely and smoothly.

The nerves that cannot be moved voluntarily are formed so you can't directly give orders to them through your cortex, which controls knowledge and conscious thought. So, your cortex makes you aware of your heartbeat, but it cannot stop it, or control the other organs. It can acknowledge the disease but can't cure it. But by practicing breathing control, you might be able to exert some control over the parts of the body controlled by the brain stem. As noted, letting a breath out for an entire minute is the objective. Everyone knows that you can't stop breathing for any extended period. But as you keep practicing, you get used to it and find it becomes easier to control. Practicing these techniques also makes your heart stronger.

I believe that right now, the only proof I have of the positive effect of multiple breathing is with the heart, but I suspect it may be beneficial for other organs as well. For example, it might be possible for people with a bad liver or intestines to practice breathing and help induce the bad condition to heal itself and go away.

The techniques for controlling both the voluntary and involuntary nerve systems of the body through breathing can also be used to control the mind. This way of thinking has been passed down from long ago and has been one of the important components used to train people in the East. The type of brain wave that you typically get with your eyes open while conscious is Type B. But when meditating with my eyes open, my brain has been generating Type A brain waves which are of a normally associated with an unconscious state.

The ability to exert control over the functions of internal organs has been proved to some extent by western science. By looking at the evidence, you can conclude that there is a way to control both the mind and the body at the same time. For instance, a method used by women to help them ease the pain of childbirth is based on multiple breathing techniques. Through these breathing techniques, the brain and the muscles relax, so the uterus becomes softer. When the body is relaxed the senses get suppressed, so the sensation of pain is reduced.

Multiple breathing directly relaxes the diaphragm, making the overall body condition relaxed. As a result, exercising becomes easier. If you get stressed, you get nervous and muscles in your shoulder and back will tighten up. When that happens, used air cannot be released and fresh air cannot come into the body. That is why it is important to relax. When you laugh or sing, your body relaxes. Comedians think about how to make audiences laugh, but it is the same as how to make them relax. The audience gets focused on the story, which makes them nervous, but when they laugh at the joke, they relax. By making them nervous, the comedian makes the audience take air in. Then when they laugh, they are made to release that air. When this process is repeated several times, the audience will surely relax until the end and will be satisfied. Audiences can practice this breathing while they are enjoying themselves.

In conclusion, by breathing more often in a conscious, focused manner, I believe that you will help yourself maintain a healthy body and mind, and help heal unhealthy conditions. I sincerely hope that you continuously practice these breathing methods.

Manual Art

Manual art means using the hands to strike, push, pull and punch the opponent, and to block attacks to vulnerable areas. Moo Yea -Do places great importance on continuous attacks, so I will do my best to explain it. You have to be consistent but also able to adapt your tactics to either defense or offense using the hands to hit or to block.

A. Standard practice

1. Stabbing with the fist
   a. In standard position, block with the front hand and hit with the other fist.
   b. Change the position and repeat.
2. Lower attack
   a. In standard position, block high attacks with the front hand and hit the neck with the lower hand.
   b. Change the position and repeat.
3. Push down and Punch

    a. In standard position, push down with the front hand and hit with the other fist.

    b. Change the position and repeat.

4. Hammer fist punch

    a. In standard position, hold or block the punch with the front hand and form a hammer fist and strike down.

    b. Change the position and repeat.

5. Back fist punch

    a. In standard position, defend with the front fist and hit with the back fist.

    b. Change the position and repeat.

6. Hitting the focus point (??)

    a. In standard position, defend your left focus point and hit the right focus point.

    b. Change the position and defend the right side and hit the left side.

7. Turn and block

    a. In standard position, block the back arm with your left arm putting it down towards inside and put your left foot out one-step and put your body towards the opponent.

    b. Change the position and repeat the process.

8. Poke the end of the hand

a. In standard position, use the front hand to block and use the back hand to attack.

b. Change the position and repeat.

9. Push and throw

a. In standard position, block with the left hand and use the right hand to go forward, and then use both hands to push the opponent.

b. Change the position and repeat.

10. Throwing the opponent overboard

When the opponent is pushing in with the hands, move the front foot to the back and make him lose the center, then, when with the hands that are pushed back, pull them over and put your left foot to make opponent fall.

11. Poking the focus point

In standard position, grab both of the fists and push the focus point down.

12. [Description ??]

In standard position, when the opponent is putting right foot in front and using the right hand for attack, block with the left hand and pull your left foot out at the same time. Put your right foot on the opponent's right side and put your right arm around the opponent's neck and when you turn left, turn your left foot 180 degrees.

B. Moo Yea-Do's basic defense system

1. Low block

2. High block

3. Middle side block

4. Middle inward block

When practicing the basic defense system, you practice 1-5 and 6-10.

1. Low block

Start from the ready position. Count one: pull your left foot next to the right foot

and protect the center with the left fist up protecting the right side of the neck, and the right fist down angling across the body. The elbows will be close together. Breathe in through the nose while moving. Count two: as the left foot steps out to the forward stance, the left arm sweeps down to block the center, while the right fist is pulled back to your right side, palm facing up. Breathe out while blocking. Count three: punch with your right fist to the middle and pull your left fist to your left side, palm up. Whenever you punch, yell (ki-hap) at the same time. Count four: pull your left foot back and put it together with the right foot. Pull both of the fists up together in front of the center of the body, palms up, while inhaling through the nose. Count five: step sideways with your left foot out to shoulder width (to return to the starting position) and push down and out with both fists with a lot of strength, while exhaling through the mouth. Count six: pull your right foot next to the left foot and protect the center with the right fist up protecting the left side of the neck, and the left fist down angling across the body. The elbows will be close together. Breathe in through the nose while moving. Count seven: as the right foot steps out to the forward stance, the right arm sweeps down to block the center, while the left fist is pulled back to your left side, palm facing up. Breathe out while blocking. Count eight: punch with your left fist to the middle and pull your right fist to your right side, palm up. Whenever you punch, yell (ki-hap) at the same time. Count nine: pull your right foot back and put it together with the left foot. Pull both of the fists up together in front of the center of the body, palms up, while inhaling through the nose. Count ten: step sideways with your right foot out to shoulder width (to return to the starting position) and push down and out with both fists with a lot of strength, while exhaling through the mouth.

2. High block

The counting is the same as with the low block. Count one: from the starting position, breathe in as you pull your left foot next to your right foot and raise your right arm to the middle center. Put your left fist, palm up, under the right elbow. Count two: as the left foot steps out to the forward stance, the left arm should be raised in front of the face and above the head to block, twisting the palm up. The left fist must be about 15 degrees higher than the elbow and the right fist is pulled back to the right side of the body, palm up. Breathe out while making this movement. Count three: pull your left fist back to the left side of your body while the right fist attacks the opponent's upper body. Yell when delivering the attack. Count four: pull your left foot back and put it together with the right foot. Pull both of the fists up together in front of the center of the body, palms up, while inhaling through the nose. Count five: step sideways with your left foot out to shoulder width (to return to the starting position) and push down and out with both fists with a lot of strength, while exhaling through the mouth. Count six: from the starting position, breathe in as you pull your right foot next to your left foot and raise your left arm to the middle center. Put your right fist, palm up, under the left elbow. Count seven: as the right foot steps out to the forward stance, the right arm should be raised in front of the face and above the head to block, twisting the palm up. The right fist must be about 15 degrees higher than the elbow and the left fist is pulled back to the left side of the body, palm up. Breathe out while making this movement. Count eight: pull your right fist back to the right side of your body while the left fist attacks the opponent's upper body. Yell when delivering the attack. Count nine: pull your right foot back and put it together with the left foot. Pull both of the fists up together in front of the center of the body, palms up, while inhaling through the nose. Count ten: step sideways with your right foot out to shoulder width (to return to the starting position) and push down and out with both fists with a lot of strength, while exhaling through the mouth.

3. Middle side block

Count one: from the starting position, breathe in as you pull your left foot next to your right foot and raise your right arm to the middle center. Put your left fist, palm down, under the right elbow. Count two: as the left foot steps out to the forward stance, the left arm held at 45 degrees passes in front of the chin and blocks the left with a circular motion. The left fist must be in a straight line with the left ear. Breathe out through the mouth as you block. At the same time, pull the right fist back to the right side of the body, palm up. Count three: pull your left fist back to the left side of the body as you attack with the right fist and yell. Count four: pull your left foot back and put it together with the right foot. Pull both of the fists up together in front of the center of the body, palms up, while inhaling through the nose. Count five: step sideways with your left foot out to shoulder width (to return to the starting position) and push down and out with both fists with a lot of strength, while exhaling through the mouth. Count six: from the starting position, breathe in as you pull your right foot next to your left foot and raise your left arm to the middle center. Put your right fist, palm down, under the left elbow. Count seven: as the right foot steps out to the forward stance, the right arm held at 45 degrees passes in front of the chin and blocks the right with a circular motion. The right fist must be in a straight line with the right ear. Breathe out through the mouth as you block. At the same time, pull the left fist back to the left side of the body, palm up. Count eight: pull your right fist back to the right side of the body as you attack with the left fist and yell. Count nine: pull your right foot back and put it together with the left foot. Pull both of the fists up together in front of the center of the body, palms up, while inhaling through the nose. Count ten: step sideways with your right foot out to shoulder width (to return to the starting position) and push down and out with both fists with a lot of strength, while exhaling through the mouth.

4. Middle inside block

Count one: from the starting position, breathe in as you pull your left foot next to your right foot and raise your right arm to the middle center. Raise your left arm with your elbow to the outside and the left palm facing forward. The left fist should be at the same height as the left ear. Count two: breathe out as the left foot steps out to the forward stance, and the left fist blocks across the face from the left ear to the level of the right ear. At the same time, pull your right fist back to the right side of the body, palm up. Count three: pull your left fist back to your left side as you attack with your right fist and yell. Count four: pull your left foot back and put it together with the right foot. Pull both of the fists up together in front of the center of the body, palms up, while inhaling through the nose. Count five: step sideways with your left foot out to shoulder width (to return to the starting position) and push down and out with both fists with a lot of strength, while exhaling through the mouth. Count six: from the starting position, breathe in as you pull your right foot next to your left foot and raise your left arm to the middle center.

Raise your right arm with your elbow to the outside and the right palm facing forward. The right fist should be at the same height as the right ear. Count seven: breathe out as the right foot steps out to the forward stance, and the right fist blocks across the face from the right ear to the level of the left ear. At the same time, pull your left fist back to the left side of the body, palm up. Count eight: pull your right fist back to your right side as you attack with your left fist and yell. Count nine: pull your right foot back and put it together with the left foot. Pull both of the fists up together in front of the center of the body, palms up, while inhaling through the nose. Count ten: step sideways with your right foot out to shoulder width (to return to the starting position) and push down and out with both fists with a lot of strength, while exhaling through the mouth.

Basic Kicking

1. Raising the leg

2. Inside swing kick

3. Inside-out kick

4. Front kick

5. Roundhouse kick

6. Side kick

7. Inside swing to reverse roundhouse kick

8. Back kick

1. Raising the leg

Count one: from the start position, jump and put your right leg back and to the right at a 45 degree angle. As you do this, both arms need to cross in front of the body to form an "X" in order to block, and then come down and out to each side (from the shoulder downward at a 45 degree angle).

Count two: raise the right leg up next to the right ear, and when you put the leg down, both arms again need to form an "X" in front of the body to block, and then come down and out to each side.

 * Change the position to the left side and repeat.

2. Inside swing kick

Count one: put your right leg back to get to the same position as raising the leg, with the same crossing two-hand down block.

Count two: put your left arm out straight with an open hand, with the palm facing right.

Count three: raise the right leg with the knee bent and swing it around toward the inside and hit the left hand. As this is done, keep the right fist on your right side, palm up.

Count four: return your right leg to the starting position.

 * Change the position to the left side and repeat.

3. Inside-out kick

Count one: again, put your right leg back to get to the same position as raising the leg, with the same crossing two-hand down block.

Count two: with the knee bent, bring your right leg up and across the body toward the left shoulder, and then circle back to the right in front of the face to return to the starting position. When you put the leg down, both arms again need to form an "X" in front of the body to block, and then come down and out to each side at a 45 degree angle.

* Change the position to the left side and repeat.

4. Front kick

Count one: from a fighting stance with the right leg back, turn your body to the front, with both of the feet facing toward the front. Keep both hands up in guard position.

Count two: raise the right knee to waist level, with the lower leg angling back toward the body at a 45 degree angle.

Count three: extend your hips and kick the opponent with the ball of the right foot (straighten your ankle with a slight inward angle to extend the ball of the foot, but flex your toes upwards so they are protected on contact).

Count four: keeping the knee up, snap your foot back toward your own body, and then return the right leg back to the starting position.

* Change the position to the left side and repeat.

5. Roundhouse kick

Count one: from a fighting stance with the right leg back, raise your right knee to the front with the foot pointing down. At the same time, pivot your left foot outward at a 45 degree angle to turn your body towards the left.

Count two: kick to the inside and hit the target with the instep of the right foot (the left foot must continue to pivot all the way as the body turns to the left).

Count three: keeping the knee up, snap your foot back toward your own body, and then return the right leg back to the starting position.

* Change the position to the left side and repeat.

6. Side kick

Count one: from a fighting stance with the right leg back, turn to the left and raise your right knee 90 degrees up and across the body; pivot your left foot so you are facing the target looking over the right shoulder. The right ankle and toes should be flexed up strongly, at an inward angle. The right arm needs to bend 90 degrees to block, and the left fist needs to be on the left side of the body with the fist facing up.

Count two: striking with the bottom of the right heel, kick the right leg to the target while pivoting your left foot toward the left (in line with your body) in order to make your kick stronger.

Count three: keeping the knee up, snap your foot back toward your own body, and then turn back to the right as you return the right leg back to the starting position.

* Change to the left side and repeat.

7. Inside swing to reverse roundhouse kick

Count one: from a fighting stance with the right leg back, kick the right leg up to the outside with a bent knee and while turning the body to the left swing the right foot across to the inside at head level, and then bring the right foot down next to the left foot.

Count two: Turning to the left and looking at the target over the left shoulder, raise the left knee at 90 degrees and kick out with the heel 45 degrees in front of the target, then hook through the target with the back of the heel while completing the turn to the left (also swinging the arms to assist the turn).

* Change to the left side and repeat.

(The inside swing kick can block the opponent's punch or kick and can be used to attack both high and low positions. The reverse roundhouse kick can be also be used to attack both high and low targets.)

8. Back kick

Count one: from a fighting stance with the right leg back, turn your upper body towards the right side, look over your right shoulder, and focus on the target. Pull your right foot back next to the left foot, keeping your knees bent. Raise your left hand and block the left side of the face; keep your right arm bent at a 90 degree angle to block.

Count two: raise your right knee with the ankle and toes flexed up strongly, and then kick straight to the target with the bottom of the right heel. Put out the right arm in the direction you are kicking.

Count three: immediately recover the kick, keeping the knee up, and turn your body back to the right in order to return the right leg to the starting position.

* Change to the left side and practice.

Basic self-defense systems

1. When the opponent grabs both of the shoulders.

    A. Cross your arms in front of your chest to form an "X" with your palms facing inward.

    B. Extend both arms out to 45 degrees, twisting the arms so that the palms of the hands face the opponent.

    C. Pull both hands back to your chest, making sure that the palms are facing toward the opponent.

    D. Step forward strongly and hit the upper chest of the opponent really hard using both hands.

2. When the opponent grabs both of the shoulders.

    A. Raise both arms to the same height as the opponent's head, with your palms together.

    B. Explosively spread your arms outward to the width of your shoulders, hitting the inner arms of the opponent.

C. Pull back and front kick the opponent.

3. When the opponent grabs both shoulders.

A. Raise the left arm towards the left ear and spread your left foot. Hit the right arm of the opponent with your left arm and put your upper body towards the right.

B. Grab the opponent's right shoulder with the left hand. Put the right arm around the opponent's neck. Turn your right foot towards left and put it around the opponent's right leg. Then push the opponent towards the left.

(Opposite direction)

C. Raise the right arm towards right ear and at the same time spread your right foot. Pull your right arm towards front and hit the left side of the opponent's left arm.

D. Grab the opponent's left shoulder with the right arm and put the left arm around the opponent's neck. Turn your left foot towards right side. At the same time, put your right leg around the left leg of the opponent and push the opponent down towards the right side

4. When the opponent grabs both shoulders.

    A. Raise the left arm and strike down the opponent's right arm at the elbow. At the same time, push up the opponent's left elbow with the right hand. Back out.

    B. Grab the opponent's right arm and put your right foot towards left. Turn and pull the opponent's right arm and push the opponent's left arm toward the right.

(Opposite direction)

    C. Raise the right arm and strike down on the opponent's left arm at the elbow. At the same time, push up the opponent's right elbow with the left hand. Back out.

    D. Grab the opponent's left arm with the right hand and turn the left foot towards the right. Turn and pull the opponent's left arm and push the opponent toward the left.

5. When the opponent grabs both shoulders.

    A. Raise the right arm and grab the opponent's right hand. Grab the left wrist of the opponent with the left hand.

    B. Put the left foot towards left side and at the same time turn the body towards the right. And pull the left hand and put it around the right arm. Push the opponent straight to his left and pull his left wrist down.

(Opposite direction)

    C. Raise the left arm and grab the opponent's left arm and with right hand, grab the opponent's right wrist.

    D. Put the right foot towards the right side and turn the body toward the left. Pull the right arm and put it around the opponent's left arm and make it up straight. Push the opponent to his right, and at the same time grab his right wrist and pull it down.

WORLD GRAND MASTER TIGER YANG'S MOO YEA-DO

KOREAN ETIQUETTE AND MASTER TERMINOLOGY

WHAT IS THE MEANING OF MOO YEA-DO?	THE WAY OF DISCIPLINE ART SIR!
WHAT IS THE PURPOSE OF MOO YEA-DO?	TO ENRICH THE LIFE OF THE INDIVIDUAL AND IMPROVE OUR SOCIETY SIR!
WHAT DO THE FUNDAMENTAL TEACHINGS OF MOO YEA-DO EMPHESIZE?	RESPECT FOR OTHERS AS LEAST AS MUCH AS AND EVEN MORE THAN FIGHTING SKILL SIR!

DEFINITIONS

Who is the founder and creator of MOO YEA-DO?	WORLD GRAND MASTER TIGER YANG SIR!!
What is the meaning of KWAN JANG NIM?	Director SIR!
Who is our KWAN JANG NIM?	Head master Paul Yang SIR!
What is the meaning of SU SUK SA BUM NIM?	Chief instructor SIR!!
What is the meaning of KYO YOUK SA BUM?	Educational instructor SIR!!
What is the meaning of JI-DO SA BUM NIM?	Chief instructor SIR!!
What is the meaning of SA BUM NIM?	Instructor SIR!!
What is the meaning of CHO-KYO?	Assistant instructor SIR!!
What is the meaning of KYO-SA?	Assistant SIR!!
What is the meaning of HWANK SANG?	Student SIR!!
What is the meaning of DO BOK?	Uniform SIR!!
What is the meaning of DO JANG?	Martial art school SIR!!!
How do you say HELLO, HOW ARE YOU?	An young hah ship knee ga,SIR!!
How do you say GOOD-BYE AND STAY WELL?	An young hee gea ship she-oh SIR!!
How do you say THANK YOU?	Kahm saamknee da SIR!!

AIM OF MOO YEA-DO

AIM OF MOO YEA-DO	MOO YEA-DO MOK JUK
RESPECT	JON KYUNG
DUTY	CHEK IM
HONOR	MYUNG YEA SIR!!!!

WORLD GRAND MASTER TIGER YANG'S MOO YEA-DO

MEANING OF MOO YEA DO

WAY OF DISCIPLINE ART

MOO (SKILL)

HOW TO DEFEND

YEA (ART)

HOW TO RESPECT

DO(PHILOSOPHY)

DISCIPLINE THE MIND & BODY

moo yea-do eui mi

Jung shin soo yang ui do

Gi sul

Ja gi bang uh

Yea yi

Jon kyung

Chui hak

Jung shin soo yang SIR!!!!

CREED

WHO ARE WE?

WHAT IS OUR GOAL?

WHAT IS OUR QUEST?

WHAT ARE WE LEARNING HERE?

GIVE ME ENERGY

WE ARE MOO YEA_DO STIJDENTS, SIR!!!

BLACK BELT EXELLENCE, SIR!!!

TO BE OUR BEST EVERYDAY, SIR

RESPECT, DUTY, HONOR!, SIR!!!

KI_OP

COUNTING IN KOREAN

1: HA NA   2: DOOL   3: SET   4: NET   5: DA SUT   6: YO SUT   7: IL KOP

8: YO DULP   9: AHOP   10: YOUL

EMPHASIS OF MENTAL TRAINING

SELF-CONTROL COMES WITH DISCIPLINE

SELF-AWARENESS COMES WITH EXPERIENCE

SELF-PEACE COMES WITH MEDITATION

SELF-CONFIDENCE COMES WITH KNOWLEDGE

SELF-SACRIFICE COMES WITH SERVICE

WORLD GRAND MASTER TIGER YANG'S MOO YEA-DO

THE FIVE D'S

DESIRE (TO DO SOMETHING) WANTING
DETERMINATION (TO DO IT) WILL
DRIVE (TO MOTIVATE YOURSELF) MOTIVATION
DEDICATION (STAY WITH IT-RESPONSIBILITY) DOGMATIC
DISCIPLINE (TO COMPLETE YOUR TASK) DESIRE IS ACTION

TEN IMPORTANT ELEMENTS OF TRAINING

CONCENTRATION
    FOCUS
    BALANCE
    POWER CONTROL
    SPEED CONTROL
    INNER CONTRL

LEVERAGE
    TIMING
    ANTICIPATION
    KI_OP

WORLD GRAND MASTER TIGER YANG'S MOO YEA-DO

COMMANDS

ENGLISH	KOREAN
ATTENTION	CHA-RYOT
READY	CHOON-BE
AT EASE	YUL CHUNG SHIY
HANDS IN THE SMALL OF BACK	
LEGS SHOULDER WITH APART	
RELAX	SHIY
BOW	KYONG REA
FORM	HYUNG
BEGIN	SEE-JAK
STOP	GU MAN
TURN AROUND	DO RA SHU
SWITCH	CHA-SE BA-GO
STRIKE	CHI-GI
KICK	CHA-GI
PUNCH	KONG KYUK
HAND	SON
STANCE	CHA-SE
BLOCK	BANG-O

WORLD GRAND MASTER TIGER YANG'S MOO YEA-DO

HAND TECHNIQUES

MIDDLE REVERSE   - CHUONG DAN KONG KYUK

HIGH PUNCH   - SANG DAN KONG KYUK

SIDE PUNCH/45°   - YUP KONG KYUK

BACKFIST   - DUONG JU MUCK

TIGER CLAW   HO JU MUCK

BEAR HAND   GOM SON

KNIFE HAND   SU DO

SPEAR HAND   KWAN SU

RIDGE HAND   YUCK SU DO

PALM STRIKE   CHANG KWON

ELBOW STRIKE   PAL GUOP CHI-GI

WORLD GRAND MASTER TIGER YANG'S MOO YEA-DO

KICKING TECHNIQUES

FRONT KICK	UP CHA-GI
ROUND HOUSE	TOLLYO CHA-GI
SIDE KICK	YUP CHA-GI
BACK KICK	DWE CHA-GI
REVERSE ROUND HOUSE	HEA CHUN CHA-GI
CRESCENT KICK	HWYI JICKACHA-GI
HOOK KICK	JICK A CHI-GI
HAMMER KICK	MANG CHI CHA-GI
HEEL KICK	DWE CHOUK CHA-GI
INSTEP KICK	BIT CHA-GI
JUMPING FRONT KICK	E-DAN UP CHA-GI
JUPING ROUNDHOUSE	D-DAN TOLLYO CHA-GI
JUMPING SIDE KICK	E-DAN YUP CHA-GI
JUMPING BACK KICK	E-DAN DWE CHA-GI
JUMPING REVERSE ROUNDHOUSE	E-DAN HEA CHUN CHA-GI
JUMPING HOOK	E-DAN JICK A CHA-GI
JUMPING CRESCENT	E-DAN HWYI TOLLYO CHA-GI

WORLD GRAND MASTER TIGER YANG'S MOO YEA-DO

STANCES

HORSE STANCE	KEE MA CHA-SE
WALKING STANCE	CHUN GUL CHA-SE
CAT STANCE	WHO GUL CHA-SE
SPARRING/FIGHTING STANCE	DAE-REN CHA-SE
TIGER/SCISSOR STANCE	HO CHA-SE
SELF DEFENSE STANCE	DO SU BANG-O CHA-SE

BLOCKS

LOW BLOCK	HA-DAN BANG-O
HIGH BLOCK	SANG-DAN YUP BANG-O
OUTSIDE BLOCK	CHUONG-DAN YUP BANG-O
INSIDE BLOCK	CHONG-DANAN BANG-O
CROSS BLOCK	SANGSOO BANG-O

TITLES

GRANDMASTER	DO SA NIM
FOUNDER AND CREATOR OF MOO YEA DO	DO JOO NIM
GRANDMASTERS WIFE	SA MO NIM
DIRECTOR	KWAN JANG NIM
CHIEF INSTRUCTOR	SU SUK SA BUM NIM
LEAD INSTRUCTOR	JI-DO SA BUM NIM
INSTRUCTOR	SA BUM NIM
ASSITANT INSTRUCTOR	CHOKYO
ASSITANT	KYOSA
SIR	NIM

WORLD GRANDMASTER TIGER YANG'S MARTIAL ART CENTER

INTERNATIONAL MOO YEA-DO FEDERATION WAY OF DISCIPLINED ART

MASTER SHEET FOR ORAL EXAMINATION AND KOREAN TERMINOLOGY

WHAT IS THE MEANING OF MOO YEA-DO?
THE WAY OF DISCIPLINED ART, SIR!

WHAT IS THE PURPOSE OF MOO YEA-DO?
TO ENRICH THE LIVES OF THE INDIVIDUAL AND TO IMPROVE OUR SOCIETY, SIR!

WHAT DO THE FUNDAMENTAL TEACHINGS OF MOO YEA-DO EMPHASIZE?
RESPECT FOR OTHERS, AT LEAST AS MUCH AS, AND EVEN MORE THAN FIGHTING
SKILLS, SIR!

ORDER RULES OF SCHOOL

BOW TO THE FLAGS AND GRANDMASTER'S OFFICE WHEN ENTERING AND LEAVING THE
STUDIO(DO JANG), SIR!

WHEN YOU SEE YOUR GRANDMASTER OR NEED TO ASK HIM A QUESTION, YOU MUST BE
RESPECTFUL, SIR!

RESPECT ALL YOUR SENIOR BELTS AND MOO YEA-DO FRIENDS, SIR!

KEEP YOUR UNIFORM AND STUDIO(DO JANG) CLEAN AT ALL TIMES, SIR!

DO NOT FACE YOUR GRANDMASTER WHEN FIXING YOUR UNIFORM, SIR!

DO NOT SMOKE, DRINK OR CHEW GUM WHILE TRAINING, SIR!

DO NOT USE PROFANITY AT ANY TIME, SIR!

DO NOT TALK OUT LOUD; NO HORSEPLAYING; NO WHISTLING, SIR!

DO NOT SPEAK TO VISITORS WHILE TRAINING, SIR!

HAVE DISCIPLINE WHILE TRAINING, SIR!

TEN COMMANDMENTS OF SELF-DEFENSE OF MOO YEA-DO

NEVER UNDERESTIMATE YOUR OPPONENT, ALWAYS ASSUME HE IS DANGEROUS, SIR!

DON'T GET FANCY, USE SIMPLE, EASY AND EFFECTIVE TECHNIQUES, SIR!

BE SURE YOU'RE ALWAYS WELL BALANCED WHEN DELIVERING A TECHNIQUE, SIR!

LEARN TO REACT INSTANTLY, BE QUICK AND ACCURATE, DO NOT HESITATE, SIR!

AFTER ATTACKING OR COUNTER-ATTACKING, NEVER LOSE SIGHT OF YOUR ADVERSARY. BE ALERT FOR CONTINUATION OF HIS ATTACK. NEVER BE CAUGHT BY SURPRISE, SIR!

ALWAYS DELIVER YOUR BLOWS TO YOUR OPPONENTS WEAKER AREAS, SIR!

ALWAYS YELL(KI-YA) WHEN DELIVERING A TECHNIQUE. THIS WILL MOMENTARILY DISTRACT AND POSSIBLY ALARM YOUR ATTACKER, SIR!

WHENEVER POSSIBLE, USA ANY AVAILABLE OBJECT AS A WEAPON TO HELP SUBDUE YOUR OPPONENT, SIR!

ALWAYS FIGHT AGGRESSIVELY, USE ALL YOUR STRENGTH, SIR!

WHEN DEFENDING YOURSELF, ALWAYS FIGHT AS IF YOUR LIFE DEPENDS ON IT. THERE IS NO TELLING WHAT YOUR ATTACKERS INTENTIONS MIGHT BE, SIR!

WORLD GRANDMASTER TIGER YANG'S MARTIAL ART CENTER

INTERNATIONAL MOO YEA-DO FEDERATION WAY OF DISCIPLINED ART

TESTING REQUIREMENTS FOR WHITE BELT(10KEUP)

PUNCHING(KONG KYUK)
- HORSE STANCE WITH MIDDLE
- REVERSE PUNCH{KEE MA CHA-SE
- CHOON-DAN KONG KYUK}
- HIGH PUNCH/SANG-DAN KONG KYUK
- SIDE PUNCH/YUP KONG KYUK

STRETCH KICKING
(AUP OLL RI GI)
- FRONT STRETCH KICK W/DOUBLE CROSS BLOCK
- AUP OLL RI GI, SANGSOO SANG-DAN BANG-0
- INSIDE/OUT STRETCH KICK W/' "
- AHNESAU PHAKOO RO OLL RIGI W/' "
- OUTSIDE/IN STRETCH KICK'
- PAHKASAU AHNOO RO OLL RIGI W/'

KICKS(CHA-GI)
- AUP CHA-GI/FRONT KICK
- TOLLYO CHA-GI/ROUNDHOUSE KICK
- YUP CHA-GI/SIDE KICK
- DWE CHA-GI/BACK KICK

STANCES(CHA-SE)
- KEE MA CHA-SE/HORSE STANCE
- CHUN GUL CHA-SE;WALKING STANCE
- WHO GUL CHA-SE/CAT STANCE
- DAE-REN CHA-SE/SPARRING STANCE
- HO CHA-SE/TIGER STANCE
- DO SU BANG-O CHA-SE/SELF DEFENSE STANCE

FORM(HYUNG)
- LOW BLOCK W/MIDDLE REVERSE PUNCH
- HA-DAN BANG-O W/CHOON-DAN KONG KYUK

- HIGH BLOCK W/HIGH PUNCH
- SANG-DAN BANG-O W/SANG-DAN KONG KYUK

- OUTSIDE BLOCK/MIDDLE REVERSE PUNCH
- CHUONG-DAN YUP '3ANG-O W/CHOON-DAN
- KONG KYUK

FORM(HYUNG)con 't   INSIDE BLOCK W/MIDDLE REVERSE PUNCH
                                CHUONG-DAN AN BANG O WI CHOON-DAN KONGKYUK

NOTE: STUDENTS UP TO AGE 14 ARE REQUIRED TO GO TO THE LEFT, TWICE. STUDENTS 15
      YEARS AND OLDER ARE REQUIRED TO GO TO THE LEFT, THEN THE RIGHT.

SELF-DEFENSE 1 THRU 5   LOW BLOCK W/ STRAIGHT PUNCH TO THE FACE
                               HIGH BLOCK W/ MIDDLE REVERSE PUNCH
                               CROSS BLOCK W/ BACK FIST
                               CROSS BLOCK W/ ELBOW STRIKE
                               CROSS BLOCK, STEP OUT W/MIDDLE REVERSE PUNCH

NOTE: SELF-DEFENSE IS DONE ON BOTH SIDES.
      STUDENTS UP TO AGE 14 ARE REQUIRED TO DO 1, 2, & 3.
      STUDENTS 15 YEARS AND OLDER ARE REQUIRED TO DO 1 THRU 5.

ORAL EXAMINATION: Q: WHAT IS THE MEANING OF *MOO YEA DO*?
                              A: THE WAY OF DISCIPLINED ART, SIR!

                              Q: WHAT IS THE PURPOSE OF *MOO YEA DO*?
                              A: TO ENRICH THE LIVES OF THE INDIVIDUAL AND TO
                                 IMPROVE OUR SOCIETY, SIR!

                              Q: WHAT DO THE FUNDAMENTAL TEACHINGS OF *MOO
                                 YEA DO* EMPHASIZE?
                              A: RESPECT FOR OTHERS, AT LEAST AS MUCH AS, AND
                                 EVEN MORE THAN FIGHTING SKILL, SIR!

                              Q: WHO IS THE FOUNDER AND CREATOR OF *MOO YEA
                                 DO*?
                              A: WORLD GRANDMASTER TIGER YANG, SIR!

                              Q: WHAT ARE YOU LEARNING HERE?
                              A: RESPECT! DUTY! HONOR!   SIR!

WORLD GRANDMASTER TIGER YANG'S MARTIAL ART CENTER

INTERNATIONAL MOO YEA-DO FEDERATION WAY OF DISCIPLINED ART

TESTING REQUIREMENTS FOR YELLOW BELT(9TH KEUP)

PUNCHING(KONG KYUK)	HORSE STANCE WITH MIDDLE
	REVERSE PUNCH{KEE MA CHA-SE
	CHOON-DAN KONG KYUK}
	HIGH PUNCH/SANG-DAN KONG KYUK
	SIDE PUNCH/YUP KONG KYUK
STRETCH KICKING	FRONT STRETCH KICK W/DOUBLE CROSS BLOCK
(AUP OLL RI GI)	AUP OLL RI GI, SANGSOO SANG-DAN BANG-0
	INSIDE/OUT STRETCH KICK Wt' "
	AHNESAU PHAKOO RO OLL RIGI W/' "
	OUTSIDE/IN STRETCH KICK Wt' "
	PAHKASAU AHNOO RO OLL RIGI Wt' "
KICKS(CHA-GI)	AUP CHA-GI/FRONT KICK
	TOLLYO CHA-GI/ROUNDHOUSE KICK
	YUP CHA-GI/SIDE KICK
	DWE CHA-GI/BACK KICK
	HEA CHUN CHA-GI/REVERSE ROUNDHOUSE KICK
STANCES(CHA-SE)	KEE MA CHA-SE/HORSE STANCE
	CHUN GUL CHA-SE/WALKING STANCE
	WHO GUL CHA-SF./CAT STANCE
	DAE-REN CHA-SE/SPARRING STANCE
	HO CHA-SE/TIGER STANCE
	DO SU BANG-O CHA-SE/SELF DEFENSE STANCE
DOUBLE BLOCKING	WHO GUL CHA-SE(CAT STANCE)
LOW, MIDDLE & HIGH	
FORM(HYUNG)	
NUNCHAKUS	

SELF-DEFENSE

NOTE: STUDENT UP TO AGE 14 ARE
REQUIRED TO DO 1, 2 & 3
STUDENTS 15 YEARS & OLDER ARE
REQUIRED TO DO 1 THROUGH 5

DAE-REN(SPARRING)

3-STEP SPARRING(VERY LIGHT CONTACT)
MALE(GROIN CUP REQUIRED)
FEMALE(CHEST PROTECTOR REQUIRED)

ORAL EXAMINATION:

WHAT IS THE MEANING OF MOO YEA-DO?
WHAT IS THE PURPOSE OF MOO YEA-DO?
WHAT DO THE FUNDAMENTAL TEACHING OF MOO YEA-
DO EMPHASIZE?
WHO IS THE FOUNDER AND CREATOR OF MOO YEA-DO?

WHAT ARE YOU LEARNING HERE?
RESPECT! DUTY! HONOR! SIR!

DESCRIBE THE FOUR TYPES
OF ATTACK:

BLOCK AND ATTACK, SIR!
FAKE AND ATTACK, SIR!
AVOID AND ATTACK, SIR!
SAME TIME ATTACK, SIR!

HOW DO YOU SAY IN KOREAN;

"HELLO, HOW ARE YOU?"

"AN YOUNG HAH SE YO?"
(INFORMAL)

"AN YOUNG HAH SHIP KNEE GA?"
(FORMAL)

THANK YOU

KAHM SAH HOP KNEE DAH

AIM OF MOO YEA DO

TESTING REQUIREMENTS FOR ORANGE BELT(8TH KEUP)

PUNCHING(KONG KYUK)	HORSE STANCE WITH MIDDLE
	REVERSE PUNCH{KEE MA CHA-SE
	CHOON-DAN KONG KYUK}
	HIGH PUNCH/SANG-DAN' KONG KYUK
	SIDE PUNCH/YUP KONG KYUK
STRETCH KICKING	FRONT STRETCH KICK W;DOUBLE CROSS BLOCK
(AUP OLL RI GI)	AUP OLL RI GI, SANGSOO SANG-DAN BANG-0
	INSIDE/OUT STRETCH KICKW/' "
	AHNESAU PHAKOO RO OLL RIG! W/' "
	OUTSIDE/IN STRETCH KICK W/' "
	PAHKASAU AHNOO RO OLL RIGI W/' "
KICKS(CHA-GI)	AUP CHA-GI/FRONT KICK
	TOLLYO CHA-GI/ROUNDHOUSE KICK
	YUP CHA-GI/SIDE KICK
	OWE CHA-GI/BACK KICK
	HEA CHUN CHA-GI/REVERSE ROUNDHOUSE KICK
STANCES(CHA-SE)	KEE MA CHA-SE/HORSE STANCE
	CHUN GUL CHA-SE/WALKING STANCE
	WHO GUL CHA-SE/C T STANCE
	DAE-REN CHA-SE/SPARRING STANCE
	HO CHA-SE/TIGER STANCE
	DO SU BANG-O CHA-SE/SELF DEFENSE STANCE
DOUBLE BLOCKING	WHO GUL CHA-SE(CAT STANCE), RETREATING
LOW, MIDDLE & HIGH	& KNEE UP
FORM(HYUNG)	
NUNCHAKUS	

SELF-DEFENSE	NOTE: STUDENT UP TO AGE 14 ARE REQUIRED TO DO 1, 2 & 3 STUDENTS 15 YEARS & OLDER ARE REQUIRED TO DO 1 THROUGH 5
DAE-REN(SPARRING)	STEP SPARRING(LIGHT/MODERATE) MALE(GROIN CUP REQUIRED) FEMALE(CHEST PROTECTOR REQUIRED)
ORAL EXAMINATION:	WHAT IS THE MEANING OF MOO YEA-DO? WHAT IS THE PURPOSE OF MOO YEA-DO? WHAT DO THE FUNDAMENTAL TEACHINGS OF MOO YEA-DO EMPHASIZE? WHO IS THE FOUNDER AND CREATOR OF MOO YEA-DO?
	WHAT ARE YOU LEARNING HERE? RESPECT! DUTY! HONOR! SIR!
DESCRIBE THE FOUR TYPES OF ATTACK:	BLOCK AND ATTACK, SIR! FAKE AND ATTACK, SIR! AVOID AND ATTACK, SIR! SAME TIME ATTACK, SIR!

HOW DO YOU SAY IN KOREAN;

GOOD BYE AND STAY WELL	AN YOUNG HEE GEA SHIP SHE-OH
HELLO, HOW ARE YOU?	"AN YOUNG HAH SHIP KNEE GA?" (FORMAL)
THANK YOU	KAHM SAH HAM KNEE DAH
KNIFE HAND	SU DO
RIDGE HAND	YUK SU DO

WORLD GRANDMASTER TIGER YANG'S MARTIAL ART CENTER

INTERNATIONAL MOO YEA-DO FEDERATION WAY OF DISCIPLINED ART

TESTING REQUIREMENTS FOR ORANGE STRIPE(8TH KEUP)

PUNCHING (KONG KYUK)	HORSE STANCE WITH MIDDLE
	REVERSE PUNCH{KEE MA CHA-SE
	CHOON-DAN KONG KYUK}
	IDGH PUNCH/SANG-DAN KONG KYUK
	SIDE PUNCH/YUP KONG KYUK
STRETCH KICKING	FRONT STRETCH KICK W/DOUBLE CROSS BLOCK
(AUP OLL RI GI)	AUP OLL RI GI, SANGSOO SANG-DAN BANG-0
	INSIDE/OUT STRETCH KICK W/' "
	AHNESAU PHAKOO RO OLL RIGI W/' "
	OUTSIDE/IN STRETCH KICK W/' "
	PAHKASAU AHNOO RO OLL RIGI W/' "
KICKS(CHA-GI)	AUP CHA-GI/FRONT KICK
	TOLLYO CHA-GI/ROUNDHOUSE KICK
	YUP CHA-GI/SIDE KICK
	DWE CHA-GI/BACK KICK
	HEA CHUN CHA-GI/REVERSE ROUNDHOUSE KICK
	CRESCENT KICK W/360° JUMPING CRESCENT
STANCES(CHA-SE)	KEE MA CHA-SE/HORSE STANCE
	CHUN GUL CHA-SE;WALKING STANCE
	WHO GUL CHA-SE/CAT STANCE
	DAE-REN CHA-SE/SPARRING STANCE
	HO CHA-SE/I'IGER STANCE
	DO SU BANG-O CHA-SE/SELF DEFENSE STANCE
DOUBLE BLOCKING	WHO GUL CHA-SE(CAT STANCE),
LOW, MIDDLE & HIGH	RETREATING & KNEE UP
HO, YOUNG, SA	TIGER, DRAGON, SNAKE
	EYE, HAND, FOOT, COORDINATION DRILL
FORM(HYUNG)	DIRECTION TO BE DETERMINED BY JUDGES

SELF-DEFENSE	NOTE: STUDENT UP TO AGE 14 ARE REQUIRED TO DO 1, 2 & 3 STUDENTS 15 YEARS & OLDER ARE REQUIRED TO DO 1 THROUGH 4
KICKING AND PUNCHING COMBINATIONS	TWO PUNCHES WITH FRONT KICK, TWO PUNCHES WITH ROUNDHOUSE KICK AND REVERSE ROUNDHOUSE KICK TWO PUNCHES WITH JUMPING FRONT KICK, FOLLOWED BY TWO PUNCHES
BREAKING REQUIREMENT	MIDDLE REVERSE PUNCH OR PALM STRIKE
ORAL EXAMINATION	WHAT IS THE MEANING OF MOO YEA-DO? WHAT IS THE PURPOSE OF MOO YEA-DO? WHAT DO THE FUNDAMENTAL TEACHINGS OF MOO YEA-DO EMPHASIZE? WHO IS THE FOUNDER AND CREATOR OF MOO YEA-DO?
	WHAT ARE YOU LEARNING HERE? RESPECT! DUTY! HONOR! SIR!
DESCRIBE THE FOUR TYPES OF ATTACK:	BLOCK AND ATTACK, SIR! FAKE AND ATTACK, SIR! AVOID AND ATTACK, SIR! SAME TIME ATTACK, SIR!

HOW DO YOU SAY IN KOREAN;

HELLO, HOW ARE YOU?	AN YOUNG HAH SE YO? (INFORMAL) AN YOUNG HAH SHIP KNEE GA? (FORMAL)
GOODBYE/STAY WELL, THANK YOU	AN YOUNG HE GEA SEH YO KAHM SAH HOP KNEE DAH

AIM OF MOO YEA-DO MEANING OF MOO YEA-DO

KNIFE HAND   SUDO
RIDGE HAND   YUCK SU DO
SPEAR HAND   KWAN SU DUONG
BACK FIST   JU MUCK

ORDER RULES OF SCHOOL 1 THROUGH 5

TESTING REQUIREMENTS FOR PURPLE BELT(7TH KEUP)

PUNCHING (KONG KYUK)	HORSE STANCE WITH MIDDLE
	REVERSE PUNCH{KEE MA CHA-SE
	CHOON-DAN KONG KYUK}
	HIGH PUNCH/SANG-DAN KONG KYUK
	SIDE PUNCH/YUP KONG KYUK
STRETCH KICKING	FRONT STRETCH KICK W/DOUBLE CROSS BLOCK
(AUP OLL RI GI)	AUP OLL RI GI, SANGSOO SANG-DAN BANG-0
	INSIDE/OUT STRETCH KICK W/' "
	AHNESAU PHAKOO RO OLL RIGI W/' "
	OUTSIDE/IN STRETCH KICK W/' "
	PAHKASAU AHNOO RO OLL RIGI W/' "
KICKS(CHA-GI)	AUP CHA-GI/FRONT KICK
	TOLLYO CHA-GI/ROUNDHOUSE KICK
	YUP CHA-GI/SIDE KICK
	OWE CHA-GI/BACK KICK
	HEA CHUN CHA-GI/REVERSE ROUNDHOUSE KICK
	CRESCENT KICK W/360° JUMPING CRESCENT
STANCES(CHA-SE)	KEE MA CHA-SE/HORSE STANCE
	CHUN GUL CHA-SE/WALKING STANCE
	WHO GUL CHA-SE/CAT STANCE
	DAE-REN CHA-SE/SPARRING STANCE
	HO CHA-SE/TIGER STANCE
	00 SU BANG-O CHA-SE/SELF DEFENSE STANCE
DOUBLE BLOCKING	WHO GUL CHA-SE(CAT STANCE), RETREATING
LOW, MIDDLE & HIGH	& KNEE UP
HO, YOUNG, SA	TIGER, DRAGON, SNAKE
	EYE, HAND, FOOT, COORDINATION DRILL
FORM(HYUNG)	

NUNCHAKUS

SELF-DEFENSE	NOTE: STUDENTUPTOAGE14ARE REQUIRED TO DO 1, 2 & 3 STUDENTS 15 **YEARS** & OLDER ARE REQUIRED TO DO 1 THROUGH 5

DAE-REN(SPARRING)	**COMBINATION SPARRING** **MEN(GROIN** CUP REQUIRED) **WOMEN(CHEST** PROTECTOR REQUIRED)

ORAL EXAMINATION:	**WHAT IS** THE **MEANING** OF MOO YEA-DO? **WHAT IS** THE **PURPOSE** OF MOO YEA-DO? **WHAT** DO THE **FUNDAMENTAL** TEACHINGS OF **MOO YEA-DO EMPHASIZE?** **WHO IS** THE FOUNDER ANO CREATOR OF **MOOYEA-00?** **WHAT ARE** YOU **LEARNING** HERE? RESPECT! DUTY! HONOR! **SIR!**

DESCRIBE THE FOUR **TYPES** OF **ATTACK:**	BLOCK **AND ATTACK, SIR!** FAKE AND ATTACK, SIR! AVOID ANO ATTACK, SIR! SAME TIME ATTACK, SIR!

HOW DO YOU SAY IN KOREAN;

HELLOW, HOW ARE YOU?	AN YOUNG HAH SE YO? (INFORMAL) AN YOUNG HAH SHIP KNEE GA? (FORMAL)
"GOOD BYE/STAY WELL"	"AN YOUNG HE GEA SEH YO."
THANK YOU	KAHM SAH HOP KNEE DAH

AIM OF MOO YEA DO

KNIFE HAND	SU DO
RIDGE HAND	YUCK SU DO
SPEAR HAND	KWAN SU

BACK FIST   DUONG JU MUCK
CRESCENT KICK HWYI TOLLYO CHA-GI

ORDER RULES OF SCHOOL 1 THOUGH 7
SELF-DEFENSE COMMANDMENTS 1,2&3

WORLD GRANDMASTER TIGER YANG'S MARTIAL ART CENTER

INTERNATIONAL MOO YEA-DO FEDERATION WAY OF DISCIPLINED ART

TESTING REQUIREMENTS FOR PURPLE STRIPE(7TH KEUP)

PUNCHING(KONG KYUK)	HORSE STANCE WITH MIDDLE
	REVERSE PUNCH{KEE MA CHA-SE
	CHOON-DAN KONG KYUK}
	HIGH PUNCH/SANG-DAN KONG KYUK
	SIDE PUNCH/YUP KONG KYUK
STRETCH KICKING	FRONT STRETCH KICK W/DOUBLE CROSS BLOCK
(AUP OLL RI GI)	AUP OLL RI GI, SANGSOO SANG-DAN BANG-O
	INSIDE/OUT STRETCH KICKW/' "
	AHNESAU PHAKOO RO Oil RIGI W/' "
	OUTSIDE/IN STRETCH KICK W/' "
	PAHKASAU AHNOO RO OLL RIGI W/' "
KICKS(CHA-GI)	AUP CHA-GI/FRONT KICK
	TOLLYO CHA-GI/ROUNDHOUSE KICK
	YUP CHA-GI/SIDE KICK
	DWE CHA-GI/BACK KICK
	HEA CHUN CHA-GI/REVERSE ROUNDHOUSE KICK
	CRESCENT KICK W/360° JUMPING CRESCENT
	DOUBLE ROUNDHOUSE KICK
STANCES(CHA-SE)	KEE MA CHA-SE/HORSE STANCE
	CHUN GUL CHA-SE/WALKING STANCE
	WHO GUL CHA-SE/CAT STANCE
	DAE-REN CHA-SE/SPARRING STANCE
	HO CHA-SE/TIGER STANCE
	00 SU BANG-O CHA-SE/SELF DEFENSE STANCE
DOUBLE BLOCKING	WHO GUL CHA-SE(CAT STANCE), RETREATING
LOW, MIDDLE & HIGH	& KNEE UP
HO, YOUNG, SA, HO, HO	TIGER, DRAGON, SNAKE
	EYE, HAND, FOOT, COORDINATION DRILL
FORM(HYUNG)	DIRECTION TO BE DETERMINED BY JUDGES
NUNCHAKUS	

SELF-DEFENSE	NOTE: STUDENT UP TO AGE 14 ARE REQUIRED TO DO 1, 2 & 3 STUDENTS 15 YEARS & OLDER ARE REQUIRED TO DO 1 THROUGH 5
KICKING AND PUNCHING COMBINATIONS	TWO PUNCHES WITH FRONT KICK, TWO PUNCHES WITH ROUNDHOUSE KICK AND REVERSE ROUNDHOUSE KICK TWO PUNCHES WITH JUMPING FRONT KICK, TWO PUNCHES WITH CRESCENT KICK AND 360° JUMPING CRESCENT KICK
BREAKING REQUIREMENT	FRONT SNAP KICK
ORAL EXAMINATION	WHAT IS THE MEANING OF MOO YEA-DO? WHAT IS THE PURPOSE OF MOO YEA-DO? WHAT DO THE FUNDAMENTAL TEACHINGS OF MOO YEA-DO EMPHASIZE? WHO IS THE FOUNDER AND CREATOR OF MOO YEA-DO? WHAT ARE YOU LEARNING HERE? RESPECT! DUTY! HONOR! SIR!
DESCRIBE THE FOUR TYPES OF ATTACK:	BLOCK AND ATTACK, SIR! FAKE AND ATTACK, SIR! AVOID AND ATTACK, SIR! SAME TIME ATTACK, SIR!

HOW DO YOU SAY IN KOREAN;

HELLO, HOW ARE YOU?	AN YOUNG HAH SE YO? (INFORMAL) AN YOUNG HAH SHIP KNEE GA? (FORMAL)
GOODBYE/STAY WELL, THANK YOU	AN YOUNG HE GEA SEH YO KAHM SAH HOP KNEE DAH

AIM OF MOO YEA DO

MEANING OF MOO YEA DO

KNIFE HAND	SU DO
RIDGE HAND	YUCK SU DO
SPEAR HAND	KWAN SU
BACK FIST	DUONG JU MUCK
CRESCENT KICK	HWYI TOLLYO CHA-GI

ORDER RULES OF SCHOOL 1-10
SELF-DEFENSE COMMNADMENTS 1-5

EMPHASIS OF MENTAL TRAINING

SELF -CONTROL COMES W/ DISCIPLINE
SELF-AWARENESS COMES W/ EXPERIENCE
SELF-PEACE COMES W/ MEDITATION
SELF-CONFIDENCE COMES W/ KNOWLEDGE
SELF-SACRIFICE COMES WI/ SERVICE

WORLD GRANDMASTER TIGER YANG'S MARTIAL ART CENTER

INTERNATIONAL MOO YEA-DO FEDERATION WAY OF DISCIPLINED ART

TESTING REQUIREMENTS FOR GREEN BELT(6TH KEUP)

PUNCHING(KONG KYUK)	HORSE STANCE WITH MIDDLE
	REVERSE PUNCH{KEE MA CHA-SE
	CHOON-DAN KONG KYUK}
	HIGH PUNCH/SANG-DAN KONG KYUK
	SIDE PUNCH/YUP KONG KYUK
STRETCH KICKING	FRONT STRETCH KICK W/DOUBLE CROSS BLOCK
(AUP OLL RI GI)	AUP OLL RI GI, SANGSOO SANG-DAN BANG-0
	INSIDE/OUT STRETCH KICKW/' "
	AHNESAU PHAKOO 1_{0 OLL RIGI W/' "
	OUTSIDE/IN STRETCH KICK W/' "
	PAHKASAU AHNOO RO OLL RIGI W/' "
KICKS(CHA-GI)	AUP CHA-GI/FRONT KICK
	TOLLYO CHA-GI/ROUNDHOUSE KICK
	YUP CHA-GI/SIDE KICK
	DWE CHA-GI/BACK KICK
	HEA CHUN CHA-GI/REVERSE ROUNDHOUSE KICK
	CRESCENT KICK W/360° JUMPING CRESCENT
	DOUBLE ROUNDHOUSE KICK
STANCES(CHA-SE)	KEE MA CHA-SE/HORSE STANCE
	CHUN GUL CHA-SE/WALKING STANCE
	WHO GUL CHA-SE/CAT STANCE
	DAE-REN CHA-SE/SPARRING STANCE
	HO CHA-SE/TIGER STANCE
	00 SU BANG-O CHA-SE/SELF DEFENSE STANCE
DOUBLE BLOCKING	WHO GUL CHA-SE(CAT STANCE), RETREATING
LOW, MIDDLE & HIGH	& KNEE UP
HO, YOUNG, SA, HO, HO	TIGER W/UP CHA-GI, DRAGON W/BIT CHA-GI &
W/CHA-GI	SNAKE W/UP CHA-GI
FORM(HYUNG)	
NUNCHAKUS	

SELF-DEFENSE

NOTE: STUDENT UP TO AGE 14 ARE
REQUIRED TO DO 1, 2 & 3
STUDENTS 15 YEARS & OLDER ARE
REQUIRED TO DO 1 THROUGH 5

DAE-REN(SPARRING)

COMBINATION SPARRING
MEN(GROIN CUP REQUIRED)
WOMEN(CHEST PROTECTOR REQUIRED)

ORAL EXAMINATION:

DESCRIBE THE FOUR TYPES OF ATTACK:

BLOCK AND ATTACK, SIR!
FAKE AND ATTACK, SIR!
AVOID AND ATTACK, SIR!
SAME TIME ATTACK, SIR!

HOW DO YOU SAY IN KOREAN;

HELLO, HOW ARE YOU?

AN YOUNG HAH SE YO? (INFORMAL)
AN YOUNG HAH SHIP KNEE GA? (FORMAL)

GOODBYE/STAY WELL,
THANK YOU

AN YOUNG HE GEA SEH YO
KAHM SAH HOP KNEE DAH

AIM OF MOO YEA DO

MEANING OF MOO YEA DO

KNIFE HAND	SU DO
RIDGE HAND	YUCK SU DO
BEAR HAND	GOM SON
SPEAR HAND	KWAN SU
BACK FIST	DUONG JU MUCK
ELBOW STRIKE	PAL GUOP CHI-GI
CRESCENT KICK	HWYI TOLLYO CHA-GI

ORDER RULES OF SCHOOL 1 THROUGH 10

COMMANDMENTS OF SELF-DEFENSE 1 THROUGH 7

IMPORTANT ELEMENTS OF TRAINING 1 THROUGH 10

EMPHASIS OF MENTAL TRAINING

SELF-CONTROL COMES W/DISCIPLINE

SELF-AWARENESS COMES W/EXPERIENCE

SELF-PEACE COMES W/MEDITATION

SELF-CONFIDENCE COMES W/KNOWLEDGE

SELF-SACRIFICE COMES W/SERVICE

TESTING REQUIREMENTS FOR GREEN STRIPE(6TH KEUP)

PUNCHING(KONG KYUK)	HORSE STANCE WITH MIDDLE
	REVERSE PUNCH{KEE MA CHA-SE
	CHOON-DAN KONG KYUK}
	IDGH PUNCH/SANG-DAN KONG KYUK
	SIDE PUNCH/YUP KONG KYUK
STRETCH KICKING	FRONT STRETCH KICK W/DOUBLE CROSS BLOCK
(AUP OLL RI GI)	AUP OLL RI GI, SANGSOO SANG-DAN BANG-0
	INSIDE/OUT STRETCH KICKW/' "
	AHNESAU PHAKOO RO OLL RIGI W/' "
	OUTSIDE/IN STRETCH KICK W/' "
	PAHKASAU AHNOO RO OLL RIGI W/' "
KICKS(CHA-GI)	AUP CHA-GI/FRONT KICK
	TOLLYO CHA-GI/ROUNDHOUSE KICK
	YUP CHA-GI/SIDE KICK
	OWE CHA-GI/BACK KICK
	HEA CHUN CHA-GI/REVERSE ROUNDHOUSE KICK
	CRESCENT KICK W/360° JUMPING CRESCENT
	DOUBLE ROUNDHOUSE KICK
STANCES(CHA-SE)	KEE MA CHA-SE/HORSE STANCE
	CHUN GUL CHA-SE/WALKING STANCE
	WHO GUL CHA-SE/CAT STANCE
	DAE-REN CHA-SE/SPARRING STANCE
	HO CHA-SE/TIGER STANCE
	DO SU BANG-O CHA-SE/SELF DEFENSE STANCE
DOUBLE BLOCKING	WHO GUL CHA-SE(CAT STANCE), RETREATING
LOW, MIDDLE & HIGH	& KNEE UP
HO, YOUNG, SA, HO, HO	TIGER W/UP CHA-GI, DRAGON W/BIT CHA-GI &
W/CHA-GI	SNAKE W/UP CHA-GI
FORM(HYUNG)	DIRECTION TO BE DETERMINED BY JUDGES
NUNCHAKUS	

SELF-DEFENSE	NOTE: STUDENT UP TO AGE 14 ARE REQUIRED TO DO 1, 2 & 3 STUDENTS 15 YEARS & OLDER ARE REQUIRED TO DO 1 THROUGH 5
KICKING AND PUNCHING COMBINATIONS	TWO PUNCHES WITH FRONT KICK, TWO PUNCHES WITH ROUNDHOUSE KICK AND REVERSE ROUNDHOUSE KICK TWO PUNCHES WITH JUMPING FRONT KICK, TWO PUNCHES WITH CRESCENT KICK AND 360° JUMPING CRESCENT KICK TWO PUNCHES WITH JUMPING ROUNDHOUSE KICK (BACK TO THE BEGINNING)
BREAKING REQUIREMENT	STEPPING SIDE KICK
ORAL EXAMINATION:	DESCRIBE THE FOUR TYPES OF ATTACK: BLOCK AND ATTACK, SIR! FAKE AND ATTACK, SIR! AVOID AND ATTACK, SIR! SAME TIME ATTACK, SIR!

HOW DO YOU SAY IN KOREAN;

HELLO, HOW ARE YOU?	AN YOUNG HAH SE YO? (INFORMAL) AN YOUNG HAH SHIP KNEE GA? (FORMAL)
GOODBYE/STAY WELL, THANK YOU	AN YOUNG HE GEA SEH YO KAHM SAH HOP KNEE DAH

AIM OF MOO YEA DO

MEANING OF MOO YEA DO

KNIFE HAND	SU DO
RIDGE HAND	YUCK SU DO
BEAR HAND	GOM SON
SPEAR HAND	KWAN SU
BACK FIST	DUONG JU MUCK
ELBOW STRIKE	PAL GUOP CHI-GI
CRESCENT KICK	HWYI TOLLYO CHA-GI
JUMPING CRESCENT KICK	E-DAN HWYI TOLLYO CHA-GI
JUMPING FRONT KICK	E-DAN UP CHA-GI
JUMPING ROUNDHOUSE KICK	E-DAN TOLLYO CHA-GI

ORDER RULES OF SCHOOL -1 THROUGH 10

COMMANDMENTS OF SELF-DEFENSE 1 THROUGH 10

IMPORTANT ELEMENTS OF TRAINING 1 THROUGH 10

EMPHASIS OF MENTAL TRAINING

SELF-CONTROL COMES W/ DISCIPLINE

SELF-AWARENESS COMES W/ EXPERIENCE

SELF-PEACE COMES W/ MEDITATION

SELF-CONFIDENCE COMES W/ KNOWLEDGE

SELF-SACRIFICE COMES WI SERVICE

TESTING REQUIREMENTS FOR BLUE BELT(5TH KEUP)

PUNCHING(KONG KYUK)

HORSE STANCE WITH MIDDLE
REVERSE PUNCH{KEE MA CHA-SE
CHOON-DAN KONG KYUK}
IDGH PUNCH/SANG-DAN KONG KYUK
SIDE PUNCH/YUP KONG KYUK

STRETCH KICKING
(AUP OLL RI GI)

FRONT STRETCH KICK W/DOUBLE CROSS BLOCK
AUP OLL RI GI, SANGSOO SANG-DAN BANG-0
INSIDE/OUT STRETCH KICKW/'   "
AHNESAU PHAKOO RO OLL RIGI W/'   "
OUTSIDE/IN STRETCH KICK W/'   "
PAHKASAU AHNOO RO OLL RIGI W/'   "

KICKS(CHA-GI)

AUP CHA-GI/FRONT KICK
TOLLYO CHA-GI/ROUNDHOUSE KICK
YUP CHA-GI/SIDE KICK
DWE CHA-GI/BACK KICK
HEA CHUN CHA-GI/REVERSE ROUNDHOUSE KICK
CRESCENT KICK W/360° JUMPING CRESCENT
DOUBLE ROUNDHOUSE KICK
JUMPING BACK KICK

STANCES(CHA-SE)

KEE MA CHA-SE/HORSE STANCE
CHUN GUL CHA-SE/WALKING STANCE
WHO GUL CHA-SE/CAT STANCE
DAE-REN CHA-SE/SPARRING STANCE
HO CHA-SE/TIGER STANCE
DO SU BANG-O CHA-SE/SELF DEFENSE STANCE

DOUBLE BLOCKING
LOW, MIDDLE & HIGH

WHO GUL CHA-SE(CAT STANCE), RETREATING
& KNEE UP

HO, YOUNG, SA, HO, HO
W/CHA-GI

TIGER W/UP CHA-GI, DRAGON W/BIT CHA-GI &
SNAKE W/UP CHA-GI

FORM(HYUNG)

NUNCHAKUS

SELF-DEFENSE	NOTE: STUDENT UP TO AGE 14 ARE REQUIRED TO DO 1, 2 & 3 STUDENTS 15 YEARS & OLDER ARE REQUIRED TO DO 1 THROUGH 4
DAE-REN(SPARRING)	FREE SPARRING(GROIN CUP, MOUTH PIECE & HEADGEAR REQUIRED)
ORAL EXAMINATION:	DESCRIBE THE FOUR TYPES OF ATTACK:

BLOCK AND ATTACK, SIR!
FAKE AND ATTACK, SIR!
AVOID AND ATTACK, SIR!
SAME TIME ATTACK, SIR!

HOW DO YOU SAY IN KOREAN;

HELLO, HOW ARE YOU?	AN YOUNG HAH SE YO? (INFORMAL) AN YOUNG HAH SHIP KNEE GA? (FORMAL)
GOODBYE/STAY WELL,	AN YOUNG HE GEA SEH YO
THANK YOU	KAHM SAH HOP KNEE DAH

AIM OF MOO YEA DO

MEANING OF MOO YEA DO

KNIFE HAND	SU DO
RIDGE HAND	YUCK SU DO
BEAR HAND	GOM SON
SPEAR HAND	KWAN SU
BACK FIST	DUONG JU MUCK
ELBOW STRIKE	PAL GUOP CHI-GI
TIGER CLAW	HOJU MUCK
CRESCENT KICK	HWYI TOLLYO CHA-GI
JUMPING CRESCENT KICK	E-DAN HWYI TOLLYO CHA-GI
JUMPING FRONT KICK	E-DAN UP CHA-GI
JUMPING ROUNDHOUSE KICK	E-DAN TOLLYO CHA-GI
JUMPING BACK KICK	E-DAN DWE CHA-GI

ORDER RULES OF SCHOOL -1 THROUGH 10

COMMANDMENTS OF SELF-DEFENSE 1 THROUGH 10

IMPORTANT ELEMENTS OF TRAINING 1 THROUGH 10

EMPHASIS OF MENTAL TRAINING

SELF-CONTROL COMES W/DISCIPLINE

SELF-AWARENESS COMES W/EXPERIENCE

SELF-PEACE COMES W/MEDITATION

SELF-CONFIDENCE COMES W/KNOWLEDGE

SELF-SACRIFICE COMES W/SERVICE

TESTING REQUIREMENTS FOR BLUE STRIPE(5TH KEUP)

PUNCHING(KONG KYUK)	HORSE STANCE WITH MIDDLE
	REVERSE PUNCH{KEE MA CHA-SE
	CROON-DAN KONG KYUK}
	HIGH PUNCWSANG-DAN KONG KYUK
	SIDE PUNCH/YUP KONG KYUK
STRETCH KICKING	FRONT STRETCH KICK W/DOUBLE CROSS BLOCK
(AUP OLL RI GI)	AUP OLL RI GI, SANGSOO SANG-DAN BANG-0
	INSIDE/OUT STRETCH KICKW/' "
	AHNESAU PHAKOO RO OLL RIGI W/' "
	OUTSIDE/IN STRETCH KICK W/' "
	PAHKASAU AHNOO RO OLL RIGI W/' "
KICKS(CHA-GI)	AUP CHA-GI/FRONT KICK
	TOLLYO CHA-GI/ROUNDHOUSE KICK
	YUP CHA-GI/SIDE KICK
	DWE CHA-GI/BACK KICK
	HEA CHUN CHA-GI/REVERSE ROUNDHOUSE KICK
	CRESCENT KICK W/360° JUMPING CRESCENT
	DOUBLE ROUNDHOUSE KICK
	JUMPING BACK KICK
STANCES(CHA-SE)	KEE MA CHA-SE/HORSE STANCE
	CHUN GUL CHA-SE/WALKING STANCE
	WHO GUL CHA-SE/CAT STANCE
	DAE-REN CHA-SE/SPARRING STANCE
	HO CHA-SE/TIGER STANCE
	DO SU BANG-O CHA-SE/SELF DEFENSE STANCE
DOUBLE BLOCKING	WHO GUL CHA-SE(CAT STANCE),
LOW, MIDDLE & HIGH	RETREATING & KNEE UP
HO, YOUNG, SA, HO, HO	TIGER W/UP CHA-GI, DRAGON W/BIT CHA-GI &
W/CHA-GI	SNAKE W/UP CHA-GI
FORM(HYUNG)	DIRECTION TO BE DETERMINED BY JUDGES

NUNCHAKUS

<u>BLUE STRIPE REQUIREMENTS CONTINUED</u>

SELF-DEFENSE	NOTE: STUDENT UP TO AGE 14 ARE REQUIRED TO DO 1, 2 & 3 STUDENTS 15 YEARS & OLDER ARE REQUIRED TO DO 1 THROUGH 4
KICKING AND PUNCHING COMBINATIONS	TWO PUNCHES WITH FRONT KICK, TWO PUNCHES WITH ROUNDHOUSE KICK AND REVERSE ROUNDHOUSE KICK TWO PUNCHES WITH JUMPING FRONT KICK, TWO PUNCHES WITH CRESCENT KICK AND 360° JUMPING CRESCENT KICK TWO PUNCHES WITH JUMPING ROUNDHOUSE KICK TWO PUNCHES WITH JUMPING SIDE KICK TWO PUNCHES WITH JUMPING REVERSE ROUNDHOUSE KICK (BACK TO THE BEGINNING)
BREAKING REQUIREMENT	REVERSE ROUNDHOUSE KICK
ORAL EXAMINATION:	DESCRIBE THE FOUR TYPES OF ATTACK: BLOCK AND ATTACK, SIR! FAKE AND ATTACK, SIR! AVOID AND ATTACK, SIR! SAME TIME ATTACK, SIR!

HOW DO YOU SAY IN KOREAN;

HELLO, HOW ARE YOU?	AN YOUNG HAH SE YO? (INFORMAL) AN YOUNG HAH SHIP KNEE GA? (FORMAL)
GOODBYE/STAY WELL, THANK YOU	AN YOUNG HE GEA SEH YO KAHM SAH HOP KNEE DAH

AIM OF MOO YEA DO

MEANING OF MOO YEA DO

KNIFE HAND	SU DO
RIDGE HAND	YUCK SU DO
BEAR HAND	GOM SON
SPEAR HAND	KWAN SU
BACK FIST	DUONG JU MUCK

ELBOW STRIKE	PAL GUOP CHI-GI
TIGER CLAW	HOJU MUCK
CRESCENT KICK	HWYI TOLLYO CHA-GI
JUMPING CRESCENT KICK	E-DAN HWYI TOLLYO CHA-GI
JUMPING FRONT KICK	E-DAN UP CHA-GI
JUMPING ROUNDHOUSE KICK	E-DAN TOLLYO CHA-GI
JUMPING BACK KICK	E-DAN DWE CHA-GI

ORDER RULES OF SCHOOL 1 THROUGH 10

COMMANDMENTSOFSEL DEFENSE1THROUGH10

IMPORTANT ELEMENTS OF TRAINING THROUGH 10

EMPHASIS OF MENTAL TRAINING

SELF-CONTROL COMES W/ DISCIPLINE

SELF-AWARENESS COMES W/ EXPERIENCE

SELF-PEACE COMES W/ MEDITATION

SELF-CONFIDENCE COMES W/ KNOWLEDGE

SELF-SACRIFICE COMES W/ SERVICE

THE FIVE D'S

DESIRE!(TO DO SOMETHING)

DETERMINATION!(TO DO IT!)

DRIVE!(TO MOTIVATE YOURSELF!)

DEDICATION!(TO STAY WITH IT! RESPONSIBILITY!)

DISCIPLINE!(TO COMPLETE YOUR TASK!)

WORLD GRANDMASTER TIGER YANG'S MARTIAL ART CENTER

INTERNATIONAL MOO YEA-DO FEDERATION WAY OF DISCIPLINED ART

TESTING REQUIREMENTS FOR BROWN BELT(4TH KEUP)

AT THE DISCRETION OF THE JUDGES, YOU CAN BE ASKED TO PERFORM ANY OR ALL OF THE PREVIOUS TECHNIQUES, FORMS OR SELF-DEFENSE

HYUNG(FORM)   BROWN BELT

NUNCHAKUS   "   "

SELF-DEFENSE   NOTE: STUDENT UP TO AGE 14 ARE
                               REQUIRED TO DO 1, 2 & 3
                               BLUE AND 1 BROWN STUDENTS 15 YEARS & OLDER ARE
                               REQUIRED TO DO 1 THROUGH 5 BLUE AND 1 BROWN

DAE-REN(SPARRING)   FREE SPARRING(FULL GEAR REQUIRED)
                               (GROIN CUP, MOUTH PIECE, HEADGEAR &
                               CHEST PROTECTOR)
                               TWO 2 MINUTE ROUNDS

ORAL EXAMINATION:

AT THE DISCRETION OF THE JUDGES YOU CAN BE ASKED ANY OR ALL OF THE PREVIOUS QUESTIONS ASKED

WORLD GRANDMASTER TIGER YANG'S MARTIAL ART CENTER

INTERNATIONAL MOO YEA-DO FEDERATION WAY OF DISCIPLINED ART

TESTING REQUIREMENTS FOR BROWN STRIPE(4TH KEUP)

AT THE DISCRETION OF THE JUDGES, YOU CAN BE ASKED TO PERFORM ANY OR ALL OF THE PREVIOUS TECHNIQUES, FORMS OR SELF-DEFENSE

HYUNG(FORM)	BROWN BELT
NUNCHAKUS	" "
SELF-DEFENSE	NOTE: STUDENT UP TO AGE 14 ARE
	REQUIRED TO DO 1, 2 & 3 BLUE AND 1 & 2 BROWN
	STUDENTS 15 YEARS & OLDER ARE REQUIRED
	TO DO 1 THROUGH 5 BLUE AND 1& 2 BROWN
KICKING AND PUNCHING	TWO PUNCHES WITH JUMPING FRONT KICK
COMBINATIONS	TWO PUNCHES WITH JUMPING ROUNDHOUSE KICK
	TWO PUNCHES WITH JUMPING SIDE KICK
BREAKING REQUIREMENT	MIDDLE REVERSE PUNCH
	STEPPING SIDE KICK
	REVERSE ROUNDHOUSE KICK

ORAL EXAMINATION:

AT THE DISCRETION OF THE JUDGES YOU CAN BE ASKED ANY OR ALL OF THE PREVIOUS QUESTIONS ASKED

TESTING REQUIREMENTS FOR RED BELT(3RD KEUP)

AT THE DISCRETION OF THE JUDGES, YOU CAN BE ASKED TO PERFORM ANY OR ALL OF THE PREVIOUS TECHNIQUES, FORMS OR SELF-DEFENSE

HYUNG(FORM)	RED BELT
NUNCHAKUS	" "
SELF-DEFENSE	NOTE: STUDENT UP TO AGE 14 ARE
	REQUIRED TO DO 1, 2 & 3 BLUE AND 1, 2 & 3 BROWN
	STUDENTS 15 YEARS & OLDER ARE REQUIRED
	TO DO 1 THROUGH 5 BLUE AND 1, 2 & 3 BROWN
DAE-REN(SPARRING)	FREE SPARRING(FULL GEAR REQUIRED)
	(GROIN CUP, MOUTH PIECE, HEADGEAR & CHEST PROTECTOR)
	TWO 2 MINUTE ROUNDS

ORAL EXAMINATION:

AT THE DISCRETION OF THE JUDGES YOU CAN BE ASKED ANY OR ALL OF THE PREVIOUS QUESTIONS ASKED

WORLD GRANDMASTER TIGER YANG'S MARTIAL ART CENTER

INTERNATIONAL MOO YEA-DO FEDERATION WAY OF DISCIPLINED ART

TESTING REQUIREMENTS FOR RED STRIPE(3RD KEUP)

AT THE DISCRETION OF THE JUDGES, YOU CAN BE ASKED TO PERFORM ANY OR ALL OF THE PREVIOUS TECHNIQUES, FORMS OR SELF-DEFENSE

HYUNG(FORM)	DIRECTION TO BE DETERMINED BY JUDGES
NUNCHAKUS	" "
SELF-DEFENSE	NOTE: STUDENT UP TO AGE 14 ARE REQUIRED TO DO 1, 2 & 3 BLUE AND 1, 2 & 3 BROWN STUDENTS 15 YEARS & OLDER ARE REQUIRED TO DO 1 THROUGH 5 BLUE AND 1, 2 & 3 BROWN
KICKING AND PUNCHING COMBINATIONS	TWO PUNCHES WITH FRONT KICK TWO PUNCHES WITH ROUNDHOUSE KICK AND REVERSE ROUNDHOUSE KICK TWO PUNCHES WITH JUMPING FRONT KICK TWO PUNCHES WITH CRESCENT KICK AND 360° CRESCENT KICK TWO PUNCHES WITH JUMPING REVERSE ROUNDHOUSE KICK TWO PUNCHES WITH JUMPING SIDE KICK TWO PUNCHES WITH JUMPING BACK KICK
BREAKING REQUIREMENT Must be done in proper order!!	Middle reverse punch Side kick Roundhouse kick Reverse roundhouse kick Jumping front kick

ORAL EXAMINATION

AT THE DISCRETION OF THE JUDGES YOU CAN BE ASKED ANY OR ALL OF THE PREVIOUS QUESTIONS ASK

TESTING REQUIREMENTS FOR CANDIDATE BLACK BELT(2ND KEUP)

STUDENTS UP TO AGE 14 ARE REQUIRED TO BE HERE TO HELP WITH TESTING IF YOU'RE NOT ALREADY TESTING

STUDENTS 15 YEARS & OLDER ARE REQUIRED TO BE HERE TO HELP WITH TESTING AND MUST LEARN HOW TO CONDUCT TESTING

AT THE DISCRETION OF THE JUDGES, YOU CAN BE ASKED TO PERFORM ANY OR ALL OF THE PREVIOUS TECHNIQUES, FORMS OR SELF-DEFENSE

HYUNG(FORM)	BROWN & RED BELT
NUNCHAKUS	PURPLE & GREEN
SELF-DEFENSE	NOTE: STUDENT UP TO AGE 14 ARE REQUIRED TO DO 1, 2, & 3 BLUE AND 1, 2, 3 & 4 BROWN STUDENTS 15 YEARS & OLDER ARE REQUIRED TO DO 1 THROUGH 5 BLUE AND 1, 2, 3 & 4 BROWN
DAE-REN(SPARRING)	FREE SPARRING(FULL GEAR REQUIRED) (GROIN CUP, MOUTH PIECE, HEADGEAR & CHEST PROTECTOR) TWO 2-MINUTE ROUNDS

ORAL EXAMINATION:

AT THE DISCRETION OF THE JUDGES YOU CAN BE ASKED ANY OR ALL OF THE QUESTIONS ASKED AT PREVIOUS RANKS

WORLD GRANDMASTER TIGER YANG'S MARTIAL ART CENTER

INTERNATIONAL MOO YEA-DO FEDERATION WAY OF DISCIPLINED ART

TESTING REQUIREMENTS FOR BLACK BELT TEST

STUDENTS UP TO AGE 14 ARE REQUIRED TO BE HERE TO HELP WITH TESTING IF YOU'RE NOT ALREADY TESTING

STUDENTS 15 YEARS & OLDER ARE REQUIRED TO BE HERE TO HELP WITH TESTING AND MUST LEARN HOW TO CONDUCT TESTING

AT THE DISCRETION OF THE JUDGES, YOU CAN BE ASKED TO PERFORM ANY OR ALL OF THE PREVIOUS TECHNIQUES, FORMS OR SELF-DEFENSE

HYUNG(FORM)   ORANGE, BLUE,BROWN & RED BELT

NUNCHAKUS   PURPLE & GREEN & FREE STYLE

NOTE: FREESTYLE NUNCHAKU HYUNG(FORM) MUST BE SUBMITTED IN WRITTEN OR TYPE
      FORM 3 DAYS BEFORE TESTING!!

SELF-DEFENSE   NOTE: STUDENT UP TO AGE 14 ARE
                    REQUIRED TO DO:
                    1, 2 & 3 ORANGE
                    1, 2 & 3 GREEN
                    1, 2 & 3 BLUE
                    1 THROUGH 4 BROWN
                    STUDENTS 15 YEARS & OLDER ARE
                    REQUIRED TO DO:
                    1 THROUGH 4 ORANGE
                    1 THROUGH 5 GREEN
                    1 THROUGH 5 BLUE
                    1 THROUGH 4 BROWN

DAE-REN(SPARRING)   FREE SPARRING(FULL GEAR REQUIRED)
                    (GROIN CUP, MOUTH PIECE, HEADGEAR & CHEST PROTECTOR)
                    TWO 2-MINUTE ROUNDS

BREAKING REQUIREMENT	Jumping front kick (E-dan up cha-gi)
Must be done in proper order!!	Jumping back kick (E-dan dwe cha-gi)
	Jumping roundhouse kick (E-dan tollyo cha-gi)
	Jumping crescent kick (E-dan hwyi tollyo cha-gi)
	Jumping reverse roundhouse kick (E-dan Hea chun cha-gi)
	Jumping side kick (E-dan yup cha-gi)

ORAL EXAMINATION:

AT THE DISCRETION OF THE JUDGES YOU CAN BE ASKED ANY OR ALL OF THE QUESTIONS ASKED AT PREVIOUS RANKS

HOW HAS MOO YEA-DO HELPED AND INFLUENCED YOUR LIFE i.e., dealing with people, work, school, family, confrontation, etc. (Example; Are you more assertive, focused, disciplined, self-confident?)

PROVIDE AT LEAST ONE PAGE, TYPED, DOUBLE SPACED. MUST BE SUBMITTED AT LEAST THREE DAYS BEFORE TESTING

GRANDMASTER'S PERSONAL HISTORY

SHOW HOW TO WRITE MOO YEA-DO, DO JOO NIM AND TIGER YANG IN KOREAN

WORLD GRANDMASTER TIGER YANG'S MARTIAL ART CENTER

INTERNATIONAL MOO YEA-DO FEDERATION WAY OF DISCIPLINED ART

Combination kicking and punching technique requirements for stripe to next belt

Orange stripe to purple: 2 punches with front kick, 2 punches with roundhouse kick and reverse roundhouse kick, 2 punches with jumping front kick, followed by 2 punches

Purple stripe to green: All of above and 2 punches with inside crescent kick and 360 degree jumping crescent kick

Green stripe to blue: All of above and 2 punches with jumping roundhouse kick

Blue stripe to brown: All of above and 2 punches with jumping side kick, and 2 punches with jumping reverse roundhouse kick

Brown stripe to red: 2 punches with jumping front kick, jumping roundhouse kick and jumping side kick

Red stripe to Candidate black belt: ALL OF ABOVE

WORLD GRANDMASTER TIGER YANG'S MARTIAL ART CENTER

INTERNATIONAL MOO YEA-DO FEDERATION WAY OF DISCIPLINED ART

BOARD BREAKING REQUIREMENTS

AGE	BOARD SIZE(WIDTH X LENGTH X THICKNESS)	BOARD TYPE
3-6	Width will vary x 12L" x 1 /4T"	Sugar Pine / White Wood
7-14	Width will vary x 12L" x 3/4T"(Actual -1/2" Thick)	Sugar Pine/ White Wood
15 & up	12W" x 12L" x 1T"(Actual - 3/4" Thick)	Ponderosa Pine / White Wood

Boards may be purchased at most hardware stores; Home Depot, Home Club, Home Base or Ganahl Lumber Co.

WORLD GRANDMASTER TIGER YANG'S MARTIAL ART CENTER

INTERNATIONAL MOO YEA-DO FEDERATION WAY OF DISCIPLINED ART

BREAKING REQUIREMENTS FOR STRIPE TO NEXT BELT

Orange stripe - Middle reverse punch

Purple stripe - Front snap kick

Green stripe - Side kick

Blue wstripe - Reverse roundhouse kick

Brown stripe - Middle reverse punch
    Stepping Side kick
    Reverse roundhouse kick

Red stripe - See below
Must be done in proper order!!

Middle reverse punch
  Step Side kick
  Roundhouse kick
  Reverse roundhouse kick
  Jumping front kick

Candidate blackbelt stripe: See below
Must be done in proper order!!

Jumping front kick
Jumping back kick
Jumping roundhouse kick
Jumping crescent kick
Jumping reverse roundhouse kick
Jumping side kick

Presidential Champion Award

90016 - 1

PRESENTED TO

International MOO YEA DO Federation
World Grand Master

TIGER YANG   1-20-2005

NAME   DATE

GOLD AWARD

In recognition of your outstanding commitment to adopt and maintain a physically active and fit lifestyle. By earning this award you have proven yourself to be a Presidential Champion.

I hereby congratulate you on this accomplishment.

Sincerely,

George W. Bush
President of the United States

The President's Challenge

The President's Challenge is a program of the President's Council on Physical Fitness and Sports, U.S. Department of Health and Human Services

Chicago 1976

. Song O. Yang, TIGER

With deepest appreciation for your generosity,

Grand Master With M.Y.D.Masters 2019

Grand Master With M.Y.D.Masters 2019

International MooYeaDo Headquarters

With President World T.K.D Fed.Dr.Cho Chung un

Grand Master Tie Honorable B.B President World T.K.D. Dr.Cho

Lee Jong Woo Kwan Jang Nim

Um un Kyu Kwan Jang Nim

with Dr. Un young Kim World T.K.D. Fed.

3rd World T.K.D. Championship at Chicago 1977

With Choi Hong Hi President. Int.T.K.D.Fed

With Hwang Ki Kwan Jang Nim

With G.master. Mas Oyama   Hong Jong Soo Kwan Jang Nim

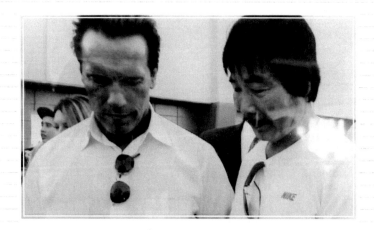

With Aranold Schwarzenegger

Ca. Lieutenant Gov. Abel Maldonado

Ca. Lieutenant Gov. Abel Maldonado

With Muhammad Ali

REGISTER

Does Tiger have one more kung-fu movie in him?

BY LORI BASHEDA
2009-03-19 03:00

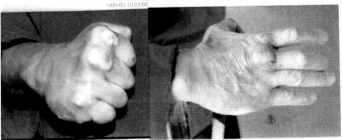

Tiger Yang, a grand master, shows off his callused hand. He has made many karate movies in in the process of of making a movie on his life. He operates a studio in Fullerton.

MARK RIGHTMIRE, THE ORANGE CO

A thousand ways to die...
Only one to live.

MASTER
INCREDIBLE

tar Productions International, Inc.

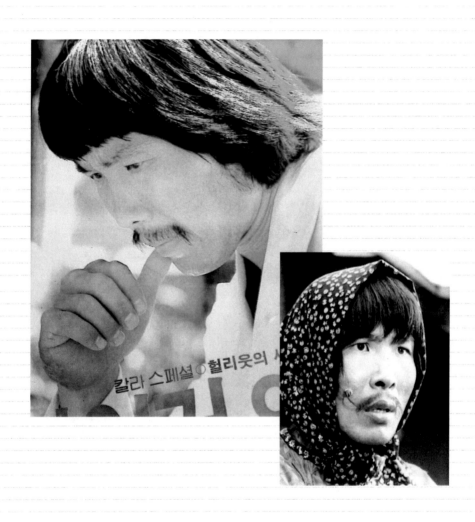

Hall of Fame With G.Master Joon Lee Washington D.C 2017

Top 2 Grand Master Best of Best World Martial Arts 2015